Gospel and Culture in Vanuatu 4

About the Editor

The Rev. Randall Prior is Professor of Ministry Studies and Missiology for the United Faculty of Theology and Director of the Uniting Church Theological College in Melbourne. He served in the Presbyterian Church of Vanuatu for five years from 1983 to 1987, in the early years following the independence of Vanuatu in 1980. He was part-time minister in the local parish of Vila and part-time resource person in education and administration for the national church.

While in Vanuatu, Randall became immersed in the challenges of the relationship between the gospel and the local cultures of the people. After his departure in 1987, Randall completed a Diploma of Mission Studies at Selly Oak Colleges in Birmingham, England, and on his return to Australia undertook a Masters Thesis on 'Gospel and Culture in Vanuatu', with a particular focus on the work of the first missionary, the Rev. John Geddie. Randall is also a graduate of the World Council of Churches' School of Ecumenical Studies at Bossey, Switzerland.

Randall has been very active in the field of gospel and culture in Australia, being instrumental in the foundation of the Commission on the Gospel and Cultures of the Victorian Council of Churches, which he chaired for its first six years. He also compiled its publication *The Gospel and Cultures: Initial Explorations in the Australian Context* (Victorian Council of Churches, 1997).

He is also the author of the first volume in the 'Gospel and Culture in Vanuatu' series, *Gospel and Culture in Vanuatu: The Founding Missionary and a Missionary for Today* (Gospel Vanuatu Books, 1998), and editor of volumes that followed, *Gospel and Culture in Vanuatu 2: Contemporary Local Perspectives* (2001) and *Gospel and Culture in Vanuatu 3: The Voice of the Local Church* (2003).

For more than two decades Randall has retained a close association with Vanuatu and remains actively involved in issues of gospel and culture, both in the South Pacific and in Australia.

The Gospel and Culture in Vanuatu series

Also available

Gospel and Culture in Vanuatu:
The Founding Missionary and a Missionary for Today
by Randall Prior

Gospel and Culture in Vanuatu 2:
Contemporary Local Perspectives
edited by Randall Prior

Gospel and Culture in Vanuatu 3:
The Voice of the Local Church
edited by Randall Prior

Gospel and Culture in Vanuatu 4

Local Voices on Jesus Christ and Mission

edited by
Randall Prior

Gospel Vanuatu Books

First published in 2005
by Gospel Vanuatu Books
6 Fowler Street
Wattle Park 3128
Australia
Telephone: +61 3 9888 7508
Email: priority49@optushome.com.au

Edited by Kevin Mark
Cover illustration by Graham Loughman
Printed in Australia by BookSurge Australia, Melbourne
ו

The National Library of Australia
Cataloguing-in-Publication Data:

Gospel and culture in Vanuatu 4 : Local voices on Jesus Christ and mission.

Bibliography.
ISBN 0 9578986 2 2

1. Christianity and culture – Vanuatu. 2. Presbyterian Church – Missions – Vanuatu. I. Prior, Randall. (Series: Gospel and culture in Vanuatu; 4).

261.099595

Brilliant Printers Pvt. Ltd., Bangalore - 94

Contents

Part One

Christology

Part Two

Mission

Part Three

Other Contemporary Issues

Introduction to the Gospel and Culture in Vanuatu Series

Since the arrival of John Geddie on the southern island of Aneityum in 1848, and the establishment of the first Christian church there, Christians have had the task of sharing the message of the gospel within the unique context of Vanuatu cultures. In the early days of Christian mission, it was generally assumed that in order to become a Christian certain basic elements of traditional culture, if not the whole culture, must be set aside and the culture of the missionaries be adopted.

In 1948, one hundred years after the arrival of John Geddie, the Presbyterian Church in these islands became an independent church – the Presbyterian Church of the New Hebrides – and this became a catalyst for the development of indigenous leadership within the local church. It was no accident that it was local church leaders who pioneered the movement that led finally to the achievement of political independence from the joint colonisers, Britain and France, in 1980. The achievement of Independence and the establishment of a locally elected indigenous parliament became a powerful impetus for the renaissance of traditional Vanuatu cultures and for the rejection of colonial cultures. This led in turn to sharper challenges for the church in matters of gospel and culture.

The question facing the church became: How can a person be faithful to the Christian gospel within their own culture? This basic question is accompanied by other related questions:
1.   If I accept the gospel, do I need to leave some or all of my culture and its practices and beliefs behind?
2.   How can the local church respond faithfully to the challenges from traditional cultural beliefs and practices?
3.   What does the gospel say about particular cultural issues facing my community?
4.   How can the church in Vanuatu continue to give leadership at the national level in the face of significant cultural changes?

Since 1980 there has been a great deal of passion given to these questions and issues; they are energetic priorities for all Christians and their church communities. However, because the cultures of Vanuatu are essentially oral cultures, there is very little that has ever been written down and made available as a resource for the local or wider public.

The 'Gospel and Culture in Vanuatu' series seeks to redress that fact. It is offered so that local people can put their ideas into print and thereby generate further local discussion, as well as giving the Vanuatu church a voice in the international missionary debate regarding gospel and culture.

This volume follows on from three earlier publications, *Gospel and Culture in Vanuatu: The Founding Missionary and a Missionary for Today* (1998), *Gospel and Culture in Vanuatu 2: Contemporary Local Perspectives* (2001) and *Gospel and Culture in Vanuatu 3: The Voice of the Local Church* (2003).

The first volume consisted of two parts: the first part examined the earliest missionary impact of the Christian gospel on the cultures of Vanuatu; the second was the pictorial representation of the Christian faith made by a talented young ni-Vanuatu man.

The second volume, a collection of interviews and workshop reports from the staff and students of the local Talua Ministry Training Centre, had the purpose of recording insights of ni-Vanuatu people about contemporary issues regarding the relationship between the Christian gospel and their own cultures, and to do so in such a way that it was the local people who were the book's authors.

The third volume was the product of a series of workshops that I was invited to run at the national assembly of the Presbyterian Church on the island of Makira in 2002. Published in time to be launched at the 2003 assembly (which marked the fiftieth anniversary of church's secondary school at Onesua), the third volume presented workshop reports from a much wider range of Presbyterian Church leaders, ordained and lay, men and women, elderly and young, across the whole island group. It also included the transcript of interviews conducted with various individuals – church leaders and chiefs. One aim of the interviews was to record the experience and wisdom of the older generation of traditional leaders – church and cultural – while it was still possible to do so.

Having duly launched the third volume in 2003, the assembly made a decision that a fourth volume be produced, and gave the task of compiling the material to their own staff at the Talua Ministry Training Centre. It also proposed that this volume focus on Christology, that is, How we understand the person and message of Jesus Christ within the context of Vanuatu cultures. So successful has the response been to this initiative that enough material has been collected for the publication of two volumes, one of which is to be ready for the 2005 assembly and the other just a few months later.

Each of the volumes in this series has marked a forward step in the process of the local church in Vanuatu taking ownership of the books, their purpose and their contents. The first book included material of my own together with the artistic representations of the Christian gospel by talented young Christian artist Graeme Loughman. The second book recorded the insights of staff and students at the Talua Ministry Training Centre gathered from a series of workshops that I ran. The third book was an extension of the second, with material gathered from a series of workshops and interviews held at the Presbyterian Church assembly at Makira Island. This fourth volume has been written, compiled and gathered by the local staff at Talua.

It remains my privilege to be a participant in the growing team of those who are engaged by the issues of gospel and culture in Vanuatu, and to facilitate the recording of the insights and ideas of the people.

Randall Prior
Series Editor

Introduction to this Volume

The publication of this volume constitutes a breakthrough in the progress of this series, indicating as it does that the local church 'owns' the project and wants to set its agenda. For this volume it has been the local people who have shouldered the responsibility of preparing and gathering the material. A working committee was established from staff members at the Talua Ministry Training Centre under the chairmanship of Father Stanley Ure from the Church of Melanesia, and it has been his committee that has done the groundwork in compiling the material.

One or two volumes?

So successful has the project been that the amount of material gathered is more than twice the material included in volume three. This posed three main problems. If we were to publish all the material into one book, the cost of purchase would be out of the reach of many people. Further, the character of the book would be very different from the previous three volumes. Finally, it became clear that the larger book would take longer to publish and so not be ready within the agreed time. For these reasons a decision was made to publish two volumes from this material, the first with a particular focus on the topics of Christology and Mission, and the second on a range of other issues including the challenging issue of women in the church.

An ecumenical venture

Another significant development is that this volume is, more obviously than the previous volumes, a publication representing perspectives and input across different traditions of the Christian church in Vanuatu. Talua is now home to staff and students from both the Presbyterian Church and the Church of Melanesia (that is, the Anglican Church) traditions, and these are well represented in this (and the projected volume to follow). There are two other 'firsts' in this volume. There is a significant contribution from a student of the Evangelical Protestant Church of Vanuatu (the *Eglise Evangelique*) and one article from the Catholic Church (by Noclam Olivier, a Tannese man who has recently graduated with a Masters Degree in Melbourne and will soon take up priesthood with the Catholic Church). It is hoped that these two developments pave the way for widening the scope of future publications in this series to represent all the traditions of the church in Vanuatu.

Editing process

Because most of the material has come to me already in writing and already in English, I have had to consider carefully the task of editing. In addition to obvious corrections in spelling and in grammar, what I have done is to make those changes that I thought were necessary in order to make the material easily understood, while at the same time preserving the content and style of the articles. This has not been a simple process – some articles required significant rewriting. However I hope I have done justice to each article and to each author. In some cases, where there were pictures or art included in the articles submitted, it has not been possible to reproduce these in the publication.

Volume four

In sorting out which material would be used for volume four and which material would be used for volume five, it became clear that priority for this volume would need to be given to those articles that clearly focused on the topic decided by the 2003 assembly, namely, the person and message of Jesus Christ in the context of Vanuatu today (Christology).

The material on Christology has been gathered into the first section of the book. It comprises a lead article from the Principal of the Talua Ministry Training Centre on 'A Christology of Hope', followed by two articles from the convener of the working committee, Father Stanley Ure – one on 'Jesus Christ as Chief' and the other on 'Jesus Christ as Healer'. The other Talua staff contribution to this section comes from Cha Jaesung from the Korean Protestant Church, who addresses the topic of the 'Universality and Particularity of the Cross in Vanuatu'. It should be noted that the original article by Cha Jaesung was much longer and more challenging to understand, and in consultation with the Talua Principal has been edited for the purposes of suitability for this publication.

The remaining articles in this section come from students who participated in a class with Father Ure on the topic of gospel and culture and addressed the question of how Jesus may be understood within their own local cultural contexts. These are primarily students who are in the lay training program or in the early stage of their ordination program. The articles are quite short and use particular local cultural symbols (for example, canoe, dolphin, yam) to represent their understanding of Jesus Christ.

The remainder of this volume falls under two headings. The first is quite directly related to Christology, namely 'Mission', that is, how the message about Jesus Christ can be communicated to other people.

Thus there are eight articles gathered under the theme of Christian mission. Shem Tamara considers the challenge to all Christians to be missionaries in their local contexts in quite practical ways. Noclam Olivier gives a Catholic Church perspective on both past and present mission, criticising mission history for its rejection of local cultures and calling on future mission to take seriously the process of inculturation. Stanley Ure's article on Justice, Peace and Love in the Pacific is an address he delivered to the second Contextual Conference of Melanesian Theologians in Honiara in 2004. John Leung, a visiting Chinese lecturer, uses his own international experience in two articles to explore the impact of globalisation on Vanuatu and the implications for the church's mission. John Richards from the Baptist tradition in Australia gives his perspective on the implications of the Christian message of forgiveness for local cultural practices of forgiveness and reconciliation. Bruce Richards, while never having been a teacher in Vanuatu, has had vast experience in mission in India; he paid a visit to Vanuatu and offers an interesting article on the relationship between the issues of gospel and culture confronted by the early church in Colossae and contemporary issues in Vanuatu. The final paper is from Cea Brian, a Church of Melanesia student who provides fascinating information about the history of the Christian mission on Mota Island in the Banks.

The third section of this volume is titled 'Other Contemporary Issues'. This is a selection of three research papers from senior students in their final year of preparation for ordination. They have been chosen because of the distinctive nature of their material. The first is by Lionel Tom, who is the first student of the French Protestant Church (*Eglise Evangelique*) to contribute to this series – his article provides insights into the history of the Protestant Church in Vanuatu and the internal tensions that now threaten it. Graham Path, a son of Doctor Titus Path (a major figure in church leadership in Vanuatu over the last fifty years), Graham tackles the vexed contemporary issue of the decline of church attendance among the youth of Vanuatu and how the church might respond. The final paper is by Church of Melanesian student William Bice Qorig from North Ambae, who explores the challenge to the church provided by the escalating social problems of urban unemployment and homelessness. These three articles were chosen from a larger pool of research articles, any number of which may have been chosen, and the remainder of which will be included in the next volume.

Thanks

Father Stanley Ure and his working committee, together with Talua Principal Pastor Masia Nato have been key resources in putting this volume together. They have given direction and encouragement for people to put their ideas onto paper. In a culture that communicates orally, this is no simple task. An unofficial part of this local Talua team has been Linda Vutilolo, secretary-typist, who has done a conscientious job in gathering and typing articles and has forwarded them to me.

A further thank you is offered to Kevin Mark who has handled the technical editing to prepare the material for publication. Kevin has worked on each of these four volumes and I have been very grateful, not only for his conscientious approach, but for his encouraging interest in my work.

A sincere word of gratitude to the Theological College of the Uniting Church in Victoria, which has contributed to the funding of this publication. The College is my new place of ministry and my colleagues there have offered generous encouragement for me to continue to pursue my keen interests in the field of gospel and culture in Vanuatu.

Upon my arrival in Vanuatu in 1983, I developed a passionate interest in the local cultures of these people and in the engagement between the Christian gospel and culture. This has continued throughout a period of over twenty years now and has had a profound influence upon my life and upon my work. I must say that at every step of the way, the people of Vanuatu have been gracious, generous and encouraging. I am particularly thankful to Fiama Rakau, Masia Nato, Kalsakau Zecharie Urtalo and Dorothy Regenvanu, local church leaders who have been colleagues and fellow-travellers in this enterprise.

Notes on the Contributors

Amanrantes Johnfred, from Bonvor, Malekula, is a Diploma 4 student of the Presbyterian Church.

Bruce Nicholls is a retired minister of the Presbyterian Church of Aotearoa New Zealand.

Cea Brian from Mota Island in the Banks is a Diploma 4 student of the Church of Melanesia.

Cha Jaesung comes from the Reformed Church of South Korea.

Christopher Iawak, from Loukatai on the island of Tanna, is a Diploma 4 student of the Presbyterian Church.

Gideon Paul, from Lorum on East Santo, is a Diploma 4 student of the Presbyterian Church.

Graham Path, from Hog Harbour on East Santo, is a Diploma 4 student of the Presbyterian Church.

John Leung was a lecturer during the 3rd term at Talua Ministry Training Centre in 2004, teaching in Biblical Studies.

John Riches [text to come]

Kalmatak Ian Tino Sope, from Mele Village on the island of Efate, is a second-year lay education student of the Presbyterian Church.

Kaltang Kai Merak, from Epau on the island of Efate, is a Diploma 4 student of the Presbyterian Church.

Kute Daniel, from Lingarak on the island of Malekula, is a Diploma 4 student of the Presbyterian Church.

Lionel Tom, from Ipayato village on South Santo, is a Diploma 4 student of the French Protestant Church.

Martin Namel, from Dillon's Bay on the island of Erromango, is a second-year lay education student from the Presbyterian Church.

Masia Nato [text to come]

Noclam Olivier [text to come]

Pastor Shem Tamara, of the Presbyterian Church of Vanuatu, is from the village of Tikilasoa on the island of Nguna, Efate. He lectures in Biblical Studies at Talua Ministry Training Centre.

Peter Lai, from Lenakel on the island of Tanna, is a Diploma 2 student of the Presbyterian Church.

Sheila Yamsiu, from Pango on the island of Efate, is a second-year lay education student of the Presbyterian Church.

Simeon Tavui, from Pelmol on South Santo, is a second-year lay education student of the Presbyterian Church.

Father Stanley Ure, from the village Aviriana, is a priest of the Church of Melanesia.

Urick Lui, from Agatoa on North Pentecost, is a second-year lay education student of the Church of Melanesia.

William Bice Qorig from Vuigalato on North Ambae is a Diploma 4 student of the Church of Melanesia.

Wilson Billy, from the island of Lelepa, is a second-year lay education student of the Presbyterian Church.

Worai Kalsakau, from Irira Island, is a second-year lay education student of the Presbyterian Church.

Part One

Christology

Christology of Hope within the Context of Vanuatu

Masia Nato

Introduction

This paper is an attempt to express the image of Christ as the source of hope within the Vanuatu context. The paper looks briefly at the background history of Vanuatu in terms of how people's lives were transformed from heathenism to Christianity, the challenges affecting the lives of the people today, and how these challenges may be overcome in today's context by reflection on Christ's image in the lives of people.

Background history

The forefathers of Vanuatu used to live a very symbolic lifestyle before the coming of the outsiders. People lived and were scattered in various mini-tribal groups. They related to each other daily. The boundaries of their tribal settlement were defined by the natural settings, the spoken languages, and the sea water encircling the islands. The tribes were tightly structured, headed by a paramount chief with other 'smaller' chiefs and their people below them. The chiefs were well respected and received by the people; when they instructed their people, the people obeyed.

People understood that their lives were surrounded by and controlled by spirits. They believed in their ancestral spirits from whom the source of power comes. In time of sickness they sought healing from the ancestral spirits; the ancestral spirits would protect them from their enemies; the ancestral spirits often brought death or caused sickness, especially if the spirits were not consulted over an issue. Much of the daily lives of the people were directed to doing things that would show appreciation of the ancestral spirits.

People spent their time gardening, hunting animals, fishing, building *nasara* (that is, a place where major ceremonies are carried out), raising pigs, participating in pig-killing ceremonies or other ceremonies related to birth, circumcision, marriages, death, et cetera. Very occasionally, they would be involved in tribal warfare for the sake of protection or retaliation.

Since the arrival of white men into Vanuatu, ni-Vanuatu lifestyle has gradually changed as people's lives were introduced to and influenced by the lifestyles of outside civilisations. A very large population of ni-Vanuatu was taken by force from their islands to the nearby countries of Australia, New Caledonia and Fiji. They were the pioneers' labourers in the large sugar cane plantations. Many returned home after their labour contracts expired, while others remained in Australia because they had come to enjoy that civilisation's lifestyle.

Coinciding with the coming of the white traders, the overseas mission churches from the Presbyterians of Scotland, Canada, Australia and New Zealand, the Anglican, the Marist Society, and later the Seventh Day Adventist, sent their missionaries to Vanuatu. They began securing land and settling missionaries on the island groups of Vanuatu, from the southern island of Aneityum to the northern islands of Banks and Torres.

The missionaries' task focused on evangelism, education and health. They evangelised the heathen people and set about planting new churches. They appointed local teachers and evangelists who ran literacy and catechist training to help people read the Scripture. Missionaries also ran health services with the aim of upgrading the living standard of the people.

A pattern occurred everywhere a missionary established a mission centre. He would invite the people from various tribal groups who were settled nearby to move closer to the mission centre. Whilst settling in the surrounding mission centre, the people attended morning and evening worship services, and both the literacy and catechist training classes. The capable students were identified and were appointed, commissioned and sent away as teacher catechists to other heathen brothers and sisters.

Many people were converted from heathenism to Christianity and abandoned their heathen beliefs. When it was the chief of a tribe who converted to Christianity, as happened occasionally, other members within his tribal group became Christians also.

In most cases missionaries cooperated well with the chiefs in reaching the heathen with the gospel. Chiefs were encouraged to abandon most of their cultural values, which were considered contrary to Christian principles. The people paid their respect to both the missionary and the chief as they were the most important and prominent figures in their community. Under their leadership people faithfully observed their duties both to their Christian belief and to their cultural values and practices. More and more people became witnesses to Christianity; the people publicly affirmed their Christian belief as it was received through the preaching and teaching of missionaries. The 'power of darkness' – as heathenism came to be known – gradually faded away.

Through the good news of the Christian gospel, the people of Vanuatu no longer lived in fear of each other; peace, love and stability prevailed as people were united under the Lordship of Christ. The development of education enabled individual Christians to read and understand God's word and to live up to the Christian standards.

In addition to the planting of Christianity throughout Vanuatu, missionary centres provided much needed health services among the people. For many years the people of Vanuatu have lived a self-subsistence lifestyle; they survive from the resources of their gardens. God has given them natural gifts such as agriculture and raising their own animals, thus economic prosperity is not an issue. They grew enough food for everyone's daily needs.

Fragmented societies

From the time when Vanuatu gained its independence from Britain and France (1980), the people of Vanuatu have gradually experienced major changes in their everyday lives. Some of these changes have assisted ni-Vanuatu to appreciate their own traditional way of living; for instance, outsiders do not need to decide what is best for the people of Vanuatu. However, to some extent, some of the changes have greatly challenged both the Christian principles and the cultural values of the people of Vanuatu. The ideal of independence has been understood in different ways. As a result, many people now seem to approach things in life in their own individual way, out of self-interest.

The two most prominent figures in communities, chiefs and pastors, have found their status challenged. People have withdrawn their trust and respect from these leaders and looked elsewhere. This has led to divisions occurring within families and communities as well as in other organisations.

Among Christians the new para-Christian groups have encouraged greater division because many people have moved away from their mainline churches and affiliated themselves with these new para-Christian groups. The leaders of these new churches have claimed that they are preaching the truth, focusing on the message of repentance, re-baptism and salvation. It is very sad that the church – which is the body of Christ and is supposed to unite the people – has instead caused ill-feeling, hatred and confusion about the teaching of the Word of God. Many Christian believers have become disturbed by the fact that their belief is questioned and challenged.

Vanuatu societies are now fragmented, not only because of the new wave of para-Christian groups, but due to other developments as well, such as in politics. In the era just before Vanuatu's independence and for a few years after independence, only two major political parties existed. The two parties helped to unite the people of Vanuatu. Today leaders of political parties with various political philosophies have established many other smaller parties for the sake of self-interest. Thus instead of people rallying behind two major parties, there are now numerous parties. These smaller political parties have taken people away from the mainline political parties and have caused more division, insecurity, disrespect and disruption. When more division occurs, there is more conflict and hatred among the people. There are many instances of unfair and unjust practices. Vanuatu's wealth is not fairly distributed. The elite, who are the politicians and the well educated, are those with good jobs and good incomes. The uneducated, with less knowledge and no jobs, are the less fortunate; their needs ignored, they struggle daily to survive. The traditional cultural value of mutual family relationship and sharing is gradually weakening. The broader community-based sharing weakens as well. The result is that each person or family cares for themselves without considering the needs of others.

Certain cultural values are challenged for the sake of economic interest. In the past, a fisherman who made a successful catch would share the fish with the whole community and a chief or pastor would be given the best fish. Such practices have disappeared. People turn to commercialisation for the fruit of their hard work; the ideologies of individualism gradually come to dominate the affairs of everyday living.

Because living in Vanuatu today is very demanding, there is worry, insecurity and instability. There is now a need to acquire income for school fees, for fulfilling chiefly duties, for church duties, for family needs, for help in times of sickness and for other commitments. When life requires greater demand, people are not free to decide for themselves the best option, but decisions are always politicised for the sake of self-interest.

Christian mission in today's society

The new challenges that Vanuatu society is facing in every level of life cannot be escaped. They cause social instability. However, if the people of Vanuatu wish to prosper again in the future, it is most important that they return to the basic Christian principles of life. These principles were laid down by pioneer missionary evangelists. The missionaries taught that faith in Jesus Christ as Lord must be a real-life experience. The people heard the Word of God that was taught and preached daily, as well as on Sundays. This Word transformed their lives. The Word made great impact and became real in the lives of the people. Even though the power of heathenism was dominant in the lives of the people, yet the Word of God proved to be greater than the power of heathenism, and it converted the people to Christianity.

When Jesus came to this world, he acknowledged the situation, the laws that forbade Jews and Gentiles to come together. In fact in the Old Testament the prophet Isaiah had already stated that the Gentiles were to be included in the Messiah's mission, and that this Messiah would restore the sight of the blind, set free the captives from prison, release from the power of evil those who sit in darkness, and proclaim justice to the nations; in his name the Gentiles would put their hope (see the quote from Isaiah in Matthew 12:18–21). Further, according to St Luke, when Jesus was a baby, he was brought to the temple, in keeping with the Jewish tradition, for dedication. Simeon, a righteous and most devout person revealed that the child would become 'a light for revelation to the Gentiles' (Luke 2:32).

These messages proclaimed by Isaiah and Simeon, show us the most important task of the Messiah, and the hope that the people expected from him. Jesus fulfilled the anticipations of the people; he demonstrated the love of God, he mingled with the outcast, he healed the sick, he restored the blind to sight. A clear example is given when Jesus meets a woman of Samaria and has a long talk with her (John 4). The woman questioned the status of Jesus as he was a Jew and she was a Samaritan, 'How is it that you, a Jew, ask a drink of me, a woman of Samaria?' (John 4:9). Jesus clearly demonstrated that he did not come for the Jews alone but for the Gentiles also, and to put an end to the dividing line that separated them. All those who believed in Jesus were to become God's children. In John 10:10 the promise offered by Jesus to all people is life to the full.

Jesus completed his ministry task through the cross on Calvary. He laid down his life for many. The apostle Paul has affirmed this message through his letter to the people of Ephesus:

> Remember that at that time you were separated from Christ, excluded from citizenship in Israel and foreigners to the covenants of promise, without hope, and without God in the world. But now in Christ Jesus, you who once were far away have been brought near through the blood of Christ. For He Himself is our Peace who has made the two one and has destroyed the barrier, the dividing wall of hostility. (Ephesians 2:12–16)

These Bible passages enable us to understand that Christ has completed the task of bringing us back into unity with him. Without heeding his words, our lives will not conform fully to the expectation and will of God. We should always acknowledge that our source of hope comes from Christ himself. When we reflect his image in our lives, we are united with him and with each other.

Through hard times, in times of sicknesses, or in times of good health, or whatever situation may challenge our lives, we must always remember that Jesus Christ is the unique source of hope for every person. Christ restores and unites us through his peace and grace and is the source of healing for the future of Vanuatu. May Christ's love and peace always prevail in our lives.

Christ our Saviour as Chief

Stanley Ure

Since that day in Caesarea Philippi when Jesus posed the question to his disciples, 'Who do the people say I am?' (Mark 8:27), the same question has been repeated to Jesus' disciples throughout the generations to this day. Anyone who becomes interested in Jesus Christ cannot avoid being challenged by the same question.

Christology has not been confined to the classical Judaeo-Hellenistic world. In recent years, contemporary Christological study is multiplying at a rapid pace. The different ways and titles by which Christ is identified by different people of different nations are never ending. In Melanesia an awareness of contextual theology is taking shape. Many serious theologians are sharing ideas and constructing their methodology of doing theology. Christology is a new intellectual exercise for Melanesia. We cannot deny people's Christology written in the page of their faith and heart. People of Melanesia have been baptised in Christ's name and also believe in him. But has Christ been identified with Melanesia, or is belief in him still in pre-formulated Western ideas? It is also common for people in need of healing to consult their local priest or pastor, believing that they can receive the healing of Jesus from them.

Some symbolic titles

Symbols and signs play a major role in Vanuatu culture and speech. One name may have several meanings (for example, a literal meaning and symbolic meanings). Birds serve as one group of symbols. There are other symbols like pig, dolphin, bow and arrow, canoe and *tam-tam*. In Vanuatu such titles are used for those who display special qualities and talents. In the Christian church, some traditional symbols are thought to represent the Holy Spirit, some represent Jesus Christ and some represent the Trinity.

Titles of Christ in Vanuatu

Here I wish to show how Christ can be addressed through the local titles by which a Vanuatu chief is addressed. These titles may be limited and short-lived yet they are the very ground of humanity in which Christ ought to be incarnated. I will look at the title of Christ the Saviour as a chief in the Vanuatu context.

When we come to ask the question, Who is a Vanuatu chief?, the answer is that he is a 'Big Man' and a rich man. When Jesus was introduced into Vanuatu, the new translation for Jesus the Saviour was *Jisas Kraes, Hae Jif blong mifala* ('Jesus Christ our Great Chief'). We believe that 'chief' is the right word to use.

Vanuatu chiefs have particular names and these names are differently known in the different societies. While the chief is the head of the community (people listen to the chief and what he says is followed), he is not better than others in the community. He stands with and for everyone in the community as a cornerstone from whom the villagers gain their support.

The chief's house (*nakamal*) is most prominent. It stands in the middle of the village. It accommodates people of different villages who come and go. It serves as a refuge for strangers caught in a heavy downpour or cyclone, or at sudden nightfall.

The chief leads in fights against the community's enemies. He may negotiate peace or an agreement in some way. He is a neutral figure who has the power to negotiate or facilitate reconciliation in conflict or disputes. He brings popularity and establishes a reputation for his tribe. On official occasions he is the one who calls his people together.

The chief possesses a special kind of gift – leadership – that attracts people. He represents his people in feasts, speeches and other important matters affecting the tribe. He is the one who decides occasions for pig-killing, young men's initiation and special dances, and oversees the ceremonies for marriages and deaths.

The chief's special gifts include ability in public speaking, wisdom, making judgement, and military skill. He is the person who establishes dialogue with all peoples and every clan.

A chief is the chief of the people and chief for the people. For all tribes, their chief is wealthy and respectable. Any son of a chief may initiate his own recognition but does so at his own risk. Those who have stepped into the shoes of their chiefly fathers are likely to acquire their father's place.

Chief Jesus Christ

I have described the qualities that the ni-Vanuatu people expect to find in their chiefs. Ni-Vanuatu do not find it difficult to apply these qualities to their 'new-found chief', Jesus.

Like any ni-Vanuatu chief, Jesus Christ was born of a woman who belonged to a family, had brothers and sisters, belonged to a tribe, was involved in rituals, was circumcised and took part in marriage ceremonies. Christ was the true chief, the perfect example of all chiefs, taking part in culture in the highest sense. Jesus can be called and compared with a fighter-warrior because he fought the common enemy of the people.

Like the Vanuatu chief who is addressed together with his tribe, so should Christ be addressed as a ni-Vanuatu Christ, a ni-Vanuatu chief. This idea of Jesus as a chief is supported in many ways by what we know of Jesus of Nazareth. Jesus was in tune with his own people. Christ represented his tribe as would a tribal chief at the feast, the sacrifice of himself. He chose to 'kill' and be himself the feast for Vanuatu so that Vanuatu people might never die. He never fought for his own survival; this is a sign of a true chief, one who stands with and for the people. He died so that others might live.

Our chief Jesus Christ is the son of no ordinary man. His chieftain-ship is inherent in the fact that it is derived directly from God. Ni-Vanuatu people know who this chief is; that is why they call him their High Chief, a good chief. He possesses all the qualities of the traditional ni-Vanuatu chief. In addition, he is no ordinary chief, his father is no ordinary man.

In Vanuatu, the chief Jesus Christ is not addressed as 'my personal Lord and Saviour', but *'our* Lord and Saviour' who stands with the people and dies for the people. To address Jesus as 'my personal Lord and Saviour' is foreign to the Vanuatu context because a chief represents his people in a tribal community in all the daily tribal activities.

In the Bible, Jesus Christ is referred to using many titles; for example, the same Christ is teacher, Son of Man, Messiah. These titles have particular meaning in the Jewish mind. In the same way, Christ appears to different people in their own languages. For Vanuatu people, it is the same story. When the Vanuatu titles are used, Christ is incarnated into the Vanuatu frame of thinking and believing, and therefore it is right that we use the word 'chief'.

Christ the Healer

Stanley Ure

In Vanuatu every year the Government spends millions of vatu on health and medical services. Schools teach about good health and hold seminars about prevention and cure of sickness in order to bring about wholeness in the lives of people. As we all know, sickness is our worst enemy because it disturbs our lives, hinders our growth and it kills many people. This presents a challenge to the ministry of the church.

Both in earlier times and today, people are in search of healing wonders; to maintain good health is of interest to everyone. During the time of Jesus we read of people who came crowding around Jesus as news of his healing miracles spread. In Vanuatu, people go from village to village to consult well-known traditional healers; sometimes they turn to the spirits of their ancestors to find the cause of sickness and suitable action that may lead to healing. The urban ni-Vanuatu will follow a similar course of action by seeking easier access to health-care services in the towns. People who are rich enough can afford the services of the best private doctors and the best hospital care.

Looking at cultural healing – The use of local medicines

In Vanuatu there are men and women who may be recognised as traditional healers. People go to their homes every day seeking their specialised help in the use of local medicines and herbs.

High blood pressure, tuberculosis, asthma, malaria and tropical ulcers all respond to traditional medicines. Bark, leaves, roots, pulp and teas – which were the basis for saving lives in the times of our ancestors, the medicines of our villages that the local physician passed on by oral tradition – are not only being revived today, they are now almost formally and officially recognised.

Even though the National Health Service is slow to legalise traditional forms of cure, each island in Vanuatu recognises the use of traditional medicines as part of our Melanesian culture. Bark and leaf medicines are of great importance in some areas that are far away from available modern health care and for those people who cannot afford hospital treatment. Importantly these medicines are readily available, are fresh and easy to digest. Ni-Vanuatu people are confident in the usefulness of traditional remedies because people in the rural villages know about them and use them to cure different kinds of sickness.

When a ni-Vanuatu healer is asked to heal a person in a village, he first goes to the patient and finds out about their sickness. Then he goes to the forest or a nearby bush area and collects the appropriate material for the curing of the sickness. When the healer approaches the tree or vine from which the material is taken for the curing of the sick, he invokes the deities to give power to the material. The belief is that the deities gave power to the material. After the invocation to the gods, the healer picks the material, converts it into juice and takes it to the patient, either for drinking or for rubbing.

In a similar way, Christian people who use local herbs for healing pray to God to ask God's blessing on the medicine, and to grant God's divine healing power to the patient.

The use of coconut oil

For the Church of Melanesia (Anglican Church) today, coconut oil is blessed by the priest or bishop and used for massage. There are some people in Vanuatu who specialise in massage. Ni-Vanuatu islanders treat massage as a kind of medical treatment, given by stroking, kneading and striking certain points of the person's body. This is used to improve blood circulation, soothe the nerves or stimulate the digestive organs. Massage helps to increase the tone of a person's muscles after a long illness. People who give the massage – Polynesian, Melanesian or Micronesian – are all well trained. They have knowledge of bone structure and human anatomy and they use their hands skilfully as they stroke on a person's muscles.

Oil in the Old Testament

In the Old Testament, we read about the use of three kinds of oil. The first is called *yishar* and it comes from the fresh oil produced by treading out the newly picked olives. This is the most highly valued and is the choicest of all the oils (Numbers 18:12); it was used for the sacred lamp stand that stood in Jerusalem (Exodus 27:20; Leviticus 24:2). It was also used for the grain offering that accompanied the twice daily corporate offering in the temple.

The second oil is called *semen*. This oil was of inferior quality, produced in larger quantities by repeating the pressing of the olive pulp. This Hebrew word is used as a general term for oil in the Bible.

The third is also called *semen*, but it is described as an anointing oil. For example this oil was used for the ordination of Aaron and his sons (Leviticus 8:2). It is also described as the holy anointing oil used to anoint the tent of the Lord's presence, the Covenant Box (Exodus 30:25). The Old Testament speaks of the anointing of kings, priests and prophets. Kings received God's power to rule over Israel and this divine selection with its reception of authority, was reflected in, for example, the anointing of Saul (1 Samuel 10:1), of David (1 Samuel 10:1–13) and Solomon (1 Kings 1:34 39). Cultic priests were also anointed, for they were selected by God and given God's authority to offer prayers and sacrifices on behalf of others (Exodus 28:41; Leviticus 6:13ff). The Bible speaks on one occasion of the literal anointing of prophets (1 Kings 19:16), but more often anointing is used to signify selection and empowerment by God (Isaiah 61:13; 1 Chronicles 6:22). Even the future deliverer of Israel was designated the Messiah, that is 'Anointed One'.

In Isaiah 1:6 oil is used as a medicine for soothing wounds. In Leviticus 14:15 18 we see the rite of the cleansing of a leper where the priest first consecrates the oil by sprinkling some of it before God, and then he applies it to the right ear, the thumb, the big toe and finally to the head of the one to be cleansed.

At the end of the mourning period, oil was used to bring joy to those in Zion who were grieving, to bring gladness instead of grief (Isaiah 61:3).

Anointing of the sick in the New Testament

In the New Testament, the anointing of the sick is mentioned in the Gospel of Mark (6:13) and in the Letter of James (5:14–15). Anointing in these instances is a means of healing, and in the James 5:14 is combined with prayer. These are the only passages in the New Testament that have a bearing on the church's practice of sacramental anointing. Both of these passages concern the use of oil in the healing of the sick. The healing with oil is the symbol of the presence and power of the Holy Spirit. This sacrament of anointing with oil gives healing both for the soul and for the body. Christ himself brought salvation and healing for the whole person, soul and body.

The anointing of Jesus as Healer

The most interesting and important aspect of anointing in the Bible is that Jesus is 'the Anointed One', the Messiah, the Christ. The significance of this is that he is the one in whom God has acted to bring healing to the peoples and to the nations. This is reflected in his own healing ministry where he heals people who have a particular sickness, but also in the fact that he brings salvation to all people. This word 'salvation' also means 'well-being' and refers to the fullness of health, the new life that Jesus has come to give to all people.

The Universality and the Particularity of the Cross in Vanuatu

Cha Jaesung

Cultural understanding of the cross in Vanuatu

Contextual theology involves three steps: (1) a passive step of understanding another context or defending our own context, (2) a rediscovering step of our own contextual value, and (3) an active step delivering our own value to another context. This process is never ignorant of or indifferent to the Christian heritage of all the saints who have been given by God as our precious treasure. We have to learn other contexts of theology throughout time and space not only to accept what other Christian sisters and brothers have done in good ways but also to correct their mistakes. Without thorough study of our Christian heritage, although it has been developed mostly in a certain area, we may not move on further. We learn not to follow but to help others.

What is the meaning of the cross in Vanuatu? As a non-ni-Vanuatu, I may not handle this question in a proper way. It is open to you all.

It is clear that the cross here in Vanuatu means mostly 'making peace by the sacrifice of the Father in his love for us and for the universe'. Moreover, the cross is understood as an event of cause and effect rather than a time-oriented happening. God the Father is comprehended as our 'Papa', the Peace-maker, and the Self-giver. Christ's work on the cross as peace-making has not been one of major themes in the history of the atonement thought except for its connection with the modern movement of non-violence or liberation theology. Thus, an accent on the cross as peacemaker would be a new emphasis for future atonement thought led by the Vanuatu context.

If peace making is an important concern here in Vanuatu, this question is significant: What would be the most serious problem of humanity?, because it is not clear whether they meant by peace-making the reconciliation between God and humanity or peace-making within humanity. According to a survey I conducted in Vanuatu, both relationships – relationship between God and humanity and the relationship between humans – were considered as equally important human problems. Obviously, the biblical understanding of love and peace encompasses both relationships; the mutual love in humanity is itself reconciliation between God and humanity (1 John 4:12). Nonetheless it is undeniable that the traditional atonement thought has put more emphasis on the reconciliation between God and humanity. It is to be noted from my survey that 79 percent of participants placed the threat of the devil in first place as the most serious human problem, whereas only 29 percent understood Christ's work as a victory over the devil. In addition, sin was seen as both a relational matter and a legal matter.

Outwardly, how can Christian believers in Vanuatu make a new and refreshed contribution to the present scholarship of the atonement thought? Their input will be highly appreciated by all believers of the world who are waiting for their help. Although I have been not able to spend enough time in collecting and encountering many stories and folktales in Vanuatu in order to find any relation between the Christian story of the cross and traditional stories in Vanuatu, I want to share several points as a refreshment and guideline for discussion.

Tam-tam

Using the *tam-tam* for calling and reconciliation would be a good example. The *tam-tam* is a traditional symbol from the northern island of Ambrym.[1] It plays three important roles: (a) calling people for meeting, (b) making peace, and (c) showing the social status of owners.[2] In the picture of the crucifixion drawn by Graham Loughman, the *tam-tam* is combined with a club used for pig killing and *namele* leaves. This is one of the stereotypes of a contextual approach to the cross: picking up different elements from the context and re-interpreting the meaning of the cross. On the one hand it tells us that the meaning of peace-making and calling all people under the cross for peace is an important aspect of the cross in Vanuatu. On the other hand, it has nothing to do with death, precisely the death by the divine being's sacrifice for humanity.

Pig-killing

Pig sacrifice is another example. It can be well connected to the cultic practice of Jewish sacrifice and other stories of sacrifice scattered all over the world. We offer animals or even human beings to the divine being and we expect to receive fortune, healing and food from the divine being in return. It is a common phenomenon that we can imagine according to the human logic of trade between what we give and what we expect to receive. A pig-killing ceremony is not connected with sacrifice in some islands of Vanuatu. Rather it is simply a banquet for celebration and reconciliation. At any rate, no true profundity of the biblical image of sacrifice can be found here. The God we believe in is the provider 'Jehovah' (Genesis 22:14) rather than the receiver of our sacrifice. The grace of God arises from God's coming in Jesus Christ even to the cross, not the other way around.

Pentecost Island

Cultural stories of the northern part of Pentecost Island are interesting in many ways.[3]

First of all, they have a precise term for the cross: *volovolo*.

> Many angels, called *Iravingaga*, came down, built a house and told a tribe with the chief whose name was Tarigesebue that they would return, so that the people in this tribe would have to wait for the angels to return. Upon their return the angels would consecrate the house. The angels made Tarigesebue promise not to kill pigs any longer. When the angels returned to this people again, they found that the people had cleaned up the place of *nasara*. Tarigesbue killed pigs and finally his brother-in-law too. The angels were angry at this and left the people, saying, 'This tribe has spoiled the cross which is called *volovolo*'. They spoiled the cross with four kinds of wind that represent human attitudes to the cross: (1) *bwatgadue*, the north wind with a bad attitude of *bwaloana* (battle), (2) *waibilage*, the south wind, with a bad attitude of *nolhoro* (anger), (3) *bwatgauna*, the east wind, with a bad attitude of *sabuana* (status of not releasing anger), and (4) *dueliu*, the west wind, with a bad attitude of *tenteneana* (denying).

I think that this may not be the end of the story of *volovolo*. We find in this story a fascinating element that *volovolo* may signify, with its four directions of wind, something of our human limitations. We can see that three elements of human problems are related to peace-making and two elements show the status of our mind. If we did some further study of the concept of sin and human misery in Pentecost Island, we may grasp a richer meaning of the cross than being over against the four winds of human limitations, since I sense that the concept of sin and human misery in this island might be very different from that in the Western world. Again, it must be observed that *volovolo* lacks the core of the Christian story of the cross, that is, the death of the divine being for humanity.

Secondly, Pentecost Island also has a human sacrifice story.

> If tribe B attacks tribe A's boundary and kills human beings and the chief of tribe A refuses to make war against tribe B, in order to restore peace the chief of tribe A has to pick one of his own men and kill him. This is all about building up peace, because the chief must do this *whether tribe A is stronger than tribe B or not* [emphasis

mine]. Killing a human being may deliver an important sign to tribe B that tribe A really wants to make peace with tribe B. This practice is called *ngarianbwaloana*.

It is not known in what way the chief is supposed to kill a man. This story of human sacrifice for making peace seems to be much more mature than common stories of cultic give-and-take sacrifice, in that it is practiced not for the sake of compensating a weak power with human sacrifice, but of making peace. In other words, even when tribe A is stronger than tribe B which attacked tribe A, tribe A holds back its power and avoids war by killing a man among its own members for the sake of peace. This story has a great affinity with the Christian cross in which God as almighty power holds back God's power and sends God's own Son, not to destroy humanity but to let God's own Son die on the cross to save humanity.

Thirdly, Pentecost Island has many other stories for peace-making: *birvia*, the name of a bird that reconciled coming battles with beautiful songs; *conato*, all living creatures that can fly; and pig-killing for making peace. These three stories, even though they are combined with the process of electing a chief, mainly concern the matter of how to make peace among different tribes. More importantly, the storyteller witnesses that people with all these stories had not been able to make true peace. They could make peace finally only by the cross of Jesus Christ. Here we may gain a tremendously important insight into the universality of the cross. The uniqueness of the cross might be the other side of the universality of the cross. Professor Viralivliv, as a Christian believer who knows all folktales and cultural stories on Pentecost Island, also witnesses that there is no story similar to the Christian cross on Pentecost Island since the cross is the Divine Being's sending of an only Son for humanity rather than receiving a sacrifice from humanity.

Conclusion

The uniqueness of the cross can be summarised in three ways: (1) the divine being is involved as the giver, (2) it is essentially about death, not something else, and (3) humankind can solve its problems by the death of the divine being.

As we have seen above, we may not find any story in Vanuatu that satisfies all three conditions. Korean folktales have many stories of the divine being's incarnation and resurrection. But there is no story of the divine being's sacrifice for humanity.

Ironically, the universality of the cross may be found not in the fact that a certain aspect of the cross can have affinity with all other stories throughout the world, but in the uniqueness that the cross cannot be shared by any other story. The cross is universal because it is unique. God loves God's creatures by God's own suffering, weakness and even death. This universal and unique truth of Christianity must not be narrowed, weakened, distorted or monopolised by any particular context. The questions of *how* and *why* this happens, however, can be enriched, re-evaluated, enforced, reformed and particularised by each context.

The true value of God's self-sacrifice in withholding God's almighty power to bring peace into our heart as well as into our daily life will be deepened in the particular context of Vanuatu. More details and richness for the universality and the particularity of the cross are open to discussion.

Bibliography

Campbell, John McLeod, *The Nature of the Atonement*, Edinburgh: The Handsel Press Ltd., 1996

Baillie, John, John T. McNeill and Henry P. Van Dusen, editors, *The Library of Christian Classics*, 26 vols., Philadelphia: Westminster Press, 1953-69

Macquarrie, John, *Jesus Christ in Modern Thought*, Philadelphia: Trinity Press International, 1990

Morris, Leon, *The Apostolic Preaching of the Cross*, 3rd ed., Grand Rapids: Eerdmans, 1994

Pannenberg, Wolfhart, *Systematic Theology*, Vol. 2, translated by Geoffrey W. Bromiley, Grand Rapids: Eerdmans, 1994

Prior, Randall, *Gospel and Culture in Vanuatu: The Founding Missionary and a Missionary for Today*, Wattle Park: Gospel Vanuatu Books, 1998

Wallace, Ronald, *The Atoning Death of Christ*, Eugene: Wipf and Stock Publishers, 1997

Jesus the Great Healer

Christopher Iawak

In our traditional culture, before the arrival of the Christian gospel, people had their own particular ways of healing. These ways were passed on from generation to generation. On the arrival of the missionaries, most of these forms of traditional medicine were considered to be related to demons, and the missionaries tried to do away with them. Even today, most of the churches give very clear teaching to their members not to use local medicine for healing. But how can we be so sure that traditional forms of local medicine are demonic without careful research into their origins and practices, and reflecting upon this in the light of the will of God as fulfilled by Jesus Christ.

Definition

The Preamble to the Constitution of the World Health Organization defines 'health' as 'a state of complete physical, mental and social well-being and not merely the absence of disease or infirmity' (http://www.who.int/about/definition).

For most Christians, the word 'healing' is related not to medicine or medical treatment but to the life of faith, to divine or spiritual healing. This springs from the view that the doctor cares for the body but the church cares for the soul. From a biblical point of view, healing actually includes the medical and non-medical, the physical and spiritual. A healer is a person who treats or provides healthy living as understood in the definition above. As a result of the fallen world, the affliction of sickness has been imposed on humankind throughout history. Our knowledge of history indicates clearly that different forms of sickness (which have prompted research, both locally and internationally, into possible cures and preventions), bring incompleteness and complication to human life.

Traditional healing

Healing is a vitally important aspect of the functioning of a society. In all cultures there is a view that people need to be healthy in order to keep the society functioning well in relation to security, providing physical needs, maintaining order and so on. Therefore there is a need to have ways of healing those who are sick. Most traditional healing or medicine comes from creation, in particular from plants.

Origins of traditional medicine

Most of the traditional medicines are handed down from generation to generation, and these are preserved and used by the society. In some ways, in our culture these medicines are related to the ancestors' gods. These gods are thought to have taught the people about many of the medicines through dreams. Others were learned by the people from their experience of nature. For example, the Tannese people who can restore a broken bone tell the story that they learned this from the example of a bird that uses part of a tree and binds it to a broken leg. This is where the practice originated that has enabled a human person to recover from a broken leg rather than face the possibility of losing a leg and so being incomplete bodily.

Often these medicines are accompanied by certain rules that will be known by the healer or medicine-maker, and must be kept by the person being healed in order for them to work successfully. The belief of our ancestors was that the rules are also kept so that the gods can bring about healing. Traditionally most of our societies are very religious and polytheistic. The people feel that they are related to their gods in a unique and intimate way.

Different kinds of sickness have different kinds of medicine, taken mainly from different kinds of plants. The sick person usually explains their sickness to the healer, who then selects a medicine that must be taken for a length of time, as required by the healer.

Biblical perspectives on healing

God who is the creator of humankind is concerned for the wholeness (health) of a person. That is why certain laws are to be kept for sound living. From the very beginning, God saw all things that God created and they were good, and God set them all under the dominion of humankind. Humankind was given the ability, skill, knowledge and creativity to relate to and use the creation for their own good (see Genesis 1 & 2, Psalm 8). People were inclined to use whatever was pleasing in creation for healing, especially leaves or parts of a plant, as in the case of Ezekiel to whom God showed which leaves to use for medical purposes (Ezekiel 47:12). The story of God showing this vision to Ezekiel indicates the familiarity of the people of those days with these concepts. (Note also a parallel in Revelation 22:2.) All that is seen by Ezekiel, especially the trees by the river bank in the temple, show that God is the source of all things in creation and humanity is to use creation while acknowledging God with a thankful heart.

Jesus the great healer

As the world moves on through different sicknesses, the people are looking forward to a time when sorrow, pain and all kinds of disease will flee away (Isaiah 29:17–19, 35:10). Isaiah prophesies of the servant who will carry the sorrow and bear the grief of his people. Matthew understands these words to be referring to the healing mission of Jesus, in which the words of Isaiah are perfectly fulfilled (Matthew 8:19). The very reason for the incarnation of Jesus was that as a perfect man 'he took up our infirmities and carried our diseases', which for Matthew does not mean that Jesus was sick, but that he was concerned about the sick and their sickness.

According to the account of Luke, Jesus came to bring about the long-awaited healing of the society (Luke 4:18–19). Again, according Matthew, Jesus' answer to John the Baptist's disciples' question as to whether he was the Messiah who was to come, was that 'the blind receive their sight, the lame walk, those who have leprosy are cleansed' (Matthew 11:5).

The ways in which Jesus approached and healed the sick are unique, for example, by his words (Mark 7:24–30), by a touch (Matthew 20:34), by having his cloak touched (Mark 5:21–29). These passages from the New Testament show that Jesus, as God himself, is the source of healing. The instance in Mark 5 where the woman simply touches the cloak of Jesus and is healed, illustrates that Jesus didn't need to use anything from creation in order to heal; he himself is the source of healing. Christ's healing ministry is clear proof that he is the great healer.

The gift of healing to the church

In the New Testament, God the Holy Spirit gives gifts for the edification of the church (1 Corinthians 12:7–10), and healing is one of these many gifts (12:9). From the record of the early history of the church recorded in Acts of the Apostles, it is clear that the disciples exercised a healing ministry through this early apostolic age (see, for example, the healing of the lame man at the temple gate in Acts 3:1–10, 5:12–16). In addition to this, we often come across cases such as Timothy who had a stomach illness (1 Timothy 5:23), and Paul himself prayed repeatedly for relief from his physical affliction, but was unsuccessful (2 Corinthians 12:7–9; Galatians 4:13–15).

These unhealed sicknesses made some people think that the gifts of healing actually ceased after a number of years. They claimed that gifts of healing were an indication of God's power and were exercised in new places, but now that we have the Bible, this gift has ceased. I do not agree with this belief because in the history of the church, including today, healing has been one of the profound aspects of the great work of God in human life. We must also understand that God answers prayer; sometimes that answer is 'yes', sometimes 'no', sometimes 'wait for a while'. Teaching about the ceasing of healing ministry in the church reduces the emphasis on healing and means that most Christians do not practice healing ministry. Some gifts are given by God in full bloom but need to be fuelled by being used (2 Timothy 1:6). Healing is one of the fundamental aspects of the life of the church, both then and now, and should also be in the future. It is a gift of the Spirit's determination (1 Corinthians 12:11) as God is the God who works in the past, the present, and will also work in the future.

A theological perspective

During the period in Vanuatu before Christianity came, our ancestors were very religious people; worship life in relation to their gods was important to them. The doctrine of God being omnipresent ('present everywhere') implies that God was in Vanuatu even before the arrival of the missionaries. The missionaries did not carry God in their vessels, but they carried the knowledge of the true living God. This means that there are some ways in which God would have been revealing God to our ancestors before the time of the missionaries, but they did not have the clear knowledge or affirmation about this God.

This brings us to the crucial question in relation to healing. Are the traditional ways of healing from God or not? Most Christians in Vanuatu today strictly forbid traditional forms of healing. Can we appreciate traditional healing in the light of the Christian gospel? Any revelation that affirms, builds and sustains life is from God the sustainer of the universe and all these revelations culminate in Jesus who perfectly fulfils all revelation. I assume that if Jesus was with our ancestors, they would not need leaves for healing because Jesus was the healer amongst them.

Now that we are taught the knowledge of fulfilment (Hebrews 1:1–3) and the true subject of our worship (Luke 24:52), this transforms the focus of our worship from other gods to the one and only true living God. Therefore, traditional healing today only has its true meaning in Jesus Christ the Healer, so that whatever I may take for healing – traditional medicine, prayer or tablets – I do it with a mind and a heart of thanksgiving that all these come from God, the source of life down through the river of history to us today. We must also know our limitations as human beings who are created body and mind with limited powers of self-healing, and know that God has placed healing agents in our environment. In modern times, some of these are offered through the practices of health professionals and come in the form of tablets. In summary, all healing is from God, whether provided through creation, providence or prayer.

The Yam as a Symbol for Jesus

Kute Daniel

Introduction

The different cultures of Vanuatu view the root crop of yam in different ways. In my own culture on Malekula Island, we regard yam as one of the most valuable items in our society. People use yam for three main purposes:

a.   as a daily food
b.   for custom ceremonies
c.   for trading – selling or exchanging

Definition

In my mother tongue, the yam is referred to as *nedam*. This is the general name for all the many types of yam, but each type of yam also has its own specific language name. These names enable us to identify the various kinds of yam we have. They were given by our ancestors as a particular way of describing each yam. Yams are also ranked according to their quality and the quality determines the value of the yam. The ranking is in three groups:

a.   King or Master yams, which are first grade
b.   Common yams, which are second grade
c.   Ordinary yams, which are third grade

Why yams are important to us

Our ancestors used yam as their main food supply in the days of our traditional cultural life. Down through the generations people lived on yams. They believed that yams gave them strength and enabled them to live longer. The main task for the community was to make sure that they planted big yam gardens to use both for food for the family and for cultural activities. Yams came to be highly valued in the lives of the people.

Custom ceremonies are very important occasions in our cultural life and on such occasions the people want to offer the very best yams that they can possibly produce in their gardens. In this way they are honoured by other members of the community and receive back from the community according to the contribution they have made to the custom ceremony.

The people use yams also as a source of income to supply their daily requirements. Yams are either sold or they are exchanged for other goods or items.

Where our yams come from

Our ancestors had a belief in the existence of many different gods. Hamashiha was the god of the seasons and Hamasdam was the god of yams. Our ancestors believed that these gods took care of them and were able to provide a good harvest for their yams. In order to have a good harvest, our people were required to pray to these gods and to ask them for a good harvest. Certain rules and rituals applied to the people in order to ensure a good yam harvest.

After the yam harvest, certain of the special yams were chosen and used as a sacrificial offering to the gods. It was the *nimbror* and *nivilbar* yams, that is, the yams ranked as King yams, that were brought as a burnt offering to the two gods, as an act of thanksgiving for the good harvest of yams.

Theologising about the cultural use of yams

1. Yam is used in all cultural ceremonies such as marriages, deaths, circumcisions, payment for punishment, and so on. When there is a custom ceremony planned for some purpose, the people are required to make sure they know about the ceremony and make time to go to their gardens in order to get a suitable yam to bring along. If people are not ready or able to bring a yam along to the ceremony, then they feel shame or guilt. Yam is the key or gateway to any custom ceremony in the culture of my people.

In considering yam in this way, the symbol of yam is suitable to represent Jesus. In John 10:9–11, Jesus says: 'I am the gate; whoever enters through me will be saved, and will come in and go out and find pasture'. Just as the yam is the means by which a local person is able to enter into our custom ceremonies, so also Jesus is the gateway to the kingdom.

2. Yam is used in the exchange of gifts in custom ceremonies. It is used as a part of the bride-price for marriage; it is used in making peace in a reconciliation ceremony involving two people or groups in conflict; it is used for payment in exchange for other valuable items, for example pigs that are also used in ceremonies. The yam is also used in the ceremonies for the ranking or promoting of people to chiefly status or title.

In this case too, the yam is a suitable symbol for Jesus. In John 14:6, Jesus says: 'I am the way, the truth and the life'. Through Jesus, there is marriage for couples, through Jesus there is reconciliation and peace, through Jesus there is payment for other necessities of life.

3. Yam is used as our main food for sustenance. It is shared with

friends, and families prepare it as food to be eaten and shared. In this way, it is important in building up strong family relationships within the community. Using the yam in this way displays our love and care for one another.

In this way again, the yam can be a symbol for Jesus who, in John 6:35 says: 'I am the bread of life'. Through Jesus there is daily food for all people in the community; through Jesus there is love and care for one another in the community.

4. Yam is used as a payment for punishment. For example, if a man is judged by the chiefs for doing wrong, he can be asked to make his payment for punishment in the form of yams. The yam becomes the key to this person's freedom.

In this sense, a yam can be a symbol for Jesus. In John 11:25, Jesus said, 'I am the resurrection and the life'. Jesus gives life and freedom in times of trouble. Even though a person dies in sin and punishment, through Jesus they will live again.

Theological meaning of yam

The yam is central to the life of our society. All people must have yam in order to participate in any cultural ceremony, to be honoured and to receive rank. This central importance of the yam makes it similar to Jesus in that it is important to have Jesus as Lord and Saviour in our lives, so that through him we will have eternal assurance of salvation (Acts 16:31). Christians are high-ranking and honoured people in our communities because they live a loving, faithful and obedient life among other people.

Yam is a plant that is planted in the ground; it grows for a long period of time and then it will produce its new fruit. The new fruit will depend very much on how well the plant grows and is looked after. When harvesting the yam, the owner will be very happy to observe the good size of the new fruit. The yam becomes the 'baby' of the ground and the ground becomes the 'mother' of the yam. We can speak of Jesus in a similar way. Jesus is the vine and his Father is the gardener or vine-dresser (John 15:1). Jesus was conceived and born of Mary his mother. Both Mary and God, his heavenly Father, took care of Jesus from a baby to an adult. Jesus spent these years with his earthly parents and then in three years completed his earthly mission. During his ministry many people were happy about all that he did and said. His teachings were good and he healed, helped and saved all kinds of needy people.

The yam flesh is planted into the ground in order to grow. It can be planted as a whole yam or a cut piece of yam. When the yam grows, the yam flesh gets rotten or decays in the ground. After some time the new yam fruit starts to grow. It continues to grow until the leaves of the yam plant become dry, then it is ready to be harvested and used. When digging the yam the owner is very happy to take it home and to share it with his family to be eaten or to use it for cultural purposes; that is the purpose of planting yams. Again there is a similarity in how we may understand Jesus. Jesus was wounded, killed and his whole body was buried in the ground. After three days he was given a new spiritual body. He went and showed himself to his disciples, then after spending some days with them, he ascended into heaven to his heavenly Father. God was pleased when Jesus completed the mission he was sent to do (Philippians 2:6–7).

Yam is sweet to eat and it is valuable to own. It is a living food because it can grow and produce more fruit. When the leaves of the yam are dry, the yam is ready to be harvested and eaten. In a similar way, Jesus is sweet to those who believe in him, and it is valuable to 'own' him in our hearts. Jesus is a growing vine and we are the branches. If we remain in him, then we too will bear new fruit in our lives. But if we do not remain in him, then he will disconnect us from himself. Then we will not bear good fruit in our lives and we will become dried up and be thrown out and burned (John 15:5–6).

Conclusion

There are many important items in our culture that we can use as symbols for Jesus. For example, *tam-tam*, bow and arrow, mat, basket, *namele* leaf, pig, turtle, white rooster, and so on. However, yam is one of the most important material items in our culture; we cannot be without yam; it is essential to our life. Without yam, we cannot participate in the life of our community and so we cannot be considered a member of our tribe. Without yam, there is no real existence. Yam is very important in our cultural context. In this paper I have tried to show how the yam can be used as an effective symbol for representing Jesus.

Note: This article is based on interviews with Chief Jacob Naus, Chief James Veve and Chief Moljung. These interviews were done in 2002 in preparation for the writing of this paper.

Jesus and the Bow and Arrow

Amanrantes Johnfred

The bow, a weapon for shooting arrows, consists of a long piece of wood bent into a curve by a string attached to both ends. The bow is the most respected weapon in my culture. Women are not permitted to touch the bow because our forefathers believed that when a woman touches a bow then it loses its sacred character and they will never be able to use that bow to shoot anything again. The bow in our tradition is treated with this sort of respect.

The use of the bow in my culture

A bow as a weapon is commonly used among my people. Male adults and children alike use the bow for hunting wild animals in the bush, shooting birds in the air and killing the fish in the sea. Wherever people go they carry a bow with them. When they go to the garden, to another village, or when they are invited to a ceremony, they always take a bow with them. Children learn how to use the bow when they are quite young; it is the first skill that the young boys learn.

There are two special cultural events where the bow is used.

Circumcision

During the celebrations of a circumcision, the children who are circumcised are required to dance with a bow and arrow; it is seen as a great honour given to the circumcised to do this. Dancing with the bow and arrow indicates that the young boys have reached a state of holiness and they are to be treated with respect by their brothers, sisters and parents.

Marriage celebration

During the marriage celebration, the man who is being married is required to carry a bow and arrow with him while performing some of the activities of the marriage ceremony, especially during the exchange of the bride-price. Marriage constitutes another development or state in the life of the man and it is a great honour for him to carry the bow and arrow.

For most adult males the bow and arrow is a part of their everyday lives. They carry the bow and arrow with them wherever they go and they use the bow and arrow as the main provider and protector. If you ask anyone why they carry their bow and arrow with them wherever they go, they will answer in this way: 'The bow and arrow is my defender and my provider'.

Defender

The bow and arrow defends people from wild animals, especially during a long journey from one village to another. On such a journey a person may be met by wild dogs or wild pigs that can attack and beat them. They use their bow to kill any threatening wild animals. The bow can also defend a person from their enemies. If a person carries a bow and arrow, then anyone who is an enemy will be afraid to do anything wrong for fear of being shot.

Provider

Men use their bow and arrow for hunting wild animals, shooting birds and killing fish. Such hunting is a common and reliable way for providing daily food for the family.

Theological perspectives

The bow and arrow can be used as a symbol for speaking about Jesus Christ. The fact that the bow and arrow is a necessity for our daily cultural life as defender and provider makes this weapon a good symbol for Jesus Christ, our defender and provider.

Christ my defender

Christ defends me from judgement. He protects me from punishment. Through Christ, God declares that I am innocent. The destroyer cannot touch the people of God (Hebrews 11:28).

Christ my provider

Jesus Christ provides me with all my daily needs. It is he who gives the rain from heaven and the crops in the garden at the right times; he gives us food and fills our hearts with happiness. Paul the apostle declares (1 Timothy 6:17) that God gives generously to us everything we need for our enjoyment (cf. Romans 8:31ff; Psalm 68:10; 111:5).

God as bow, Jesus as arrow

It is possible in one sense to speak of God as a bow and of Jesus as an arrow. The two depend upon each other, the arrow cannot be sent without the bow; they both relate to each other; the bow is regarded as holy. We pray to God and God responds to our prayers through Jesus Christ. God sent Jesus in order to destroy Satan and make us safe. We are blessed through Jesus. He is the defender and provider for our daily living.

Who is Jesus? ... Son of God according to the Scriptures

Kaltang Kai Merak

First I would like us to consider the Trinity. The Bible teaches us that while God is one, he exists in three persons, the Father, the Son and the Holy Spirit. These are not three persons in the ordinary sense of the word; they are not three individuals but rather three modes or forms in which the Divine Being exists. At the same time they are of such a nature that they can enter into personal relations.

The progress of revelation in the New Testament sets it out clearly. In the beginning the Word already existed (John 1:1); the Word came into the world revealing God to humankind. When we think of the second person of the Trinity, referred to as the Son, we learn that he is the only begotten of the Father but is also known as the Messiah, the anointed one of God who generates the Son from eternity. The Son does the work ascribed to him, the work of redemption, and represents the Trinity in this work of redemption (Berkhof, pp. 38–9).

The Bible represents Jesus Christ as a person with two natures, the one 'divine' and the other 'human'. This is the great mystery of godliness among us, God in the flesh (1 Timothy 3:16).

Since many in our day deny the deity of Christ, it is good to see the scriptural proof for this deity: Isaiah 9:6, Jeremiah 23:6, Micah 5:2 and Malachi 3:1 all point to the deity of the Son of God. The humanity of Jesus is not called into question; in fact the only divinity that is ascribed to him is that he is perfectly human. There is abundant proof of the humanity of Jesus in the Scriptures. Jesus speaks of himself as human (John 8:40) and is spoken of by others as human with both body and soul (Matthew 26:26–38). He was subject to the ordinary processes of human development (Luke 2:4) and experienced human wants and human sufferings (Matthew 4:2). Although he was truly human, Jesus was without sin (Berkhof, pp. 86–7).

The two natures of Christ are united in the one person of Christ. Christ has a human nature but he is unique. In the incarnation, he who was already divine assumed a human nature that did not exist independently of his divinity, but was united in this Son of God. Therefore when we think of Jesus who is in the bosom of the Father, we understand that he became human as the Word of God (John 1:1–3, 14–18). The apostle Paul wrote about the 'pre-existence of Jesus'; the gospel writer John emphasises this more strongly than any other New Testament writer, namely that he was in the beginning with God and was God (John 1:1f).

After Jesus' assumption of human nature, the person of the mediator is not only divine, but also human. He is the God-man, possessing all the essential qualities of both the human and the divine natures.

The following presents some of the proof from Scripture that Jesus, as a human person in the world, is really the Son of God. The miracles he performs are probably the most important signs that he is the Son of God.

Water into wine (John 2:1–11)

Jesus performs this miracle as a human person while he was present with members of his family at a wedding feast. He instructed the stewards to fill the jars with water and then, taking the lid off, they discovered it had become wine.

Feeding the five thousand (Matthew 14:15–21)

Jesus told his disciples to bring the two fish and five loaves of bread to him; he took them and told his disciples to order the crowd to sit down; he gave thanks and broke the bread. The disciples took the bread and the fish and fed the people. After everyone had eaten, there were enough leftovers to fill twelve baskets.

Raising a person from the dead (Luke 7:11–17)

Jesus raises the only son of a widow in front of a large crowd in the city of Nain. As the people carried the man out in a coffin, Jesus had compassion on the widow; he touched the coffin and said to the man to rise. The dead man sat up and spoke and Jesus gave him back to his mother. The crowd was amazed and realised that Jesus was a servant of God.

Walking on water (Matthew 14:24–33)

Jesus walked on water towards his disciples and they were afraid because they thought it was a ghost. But Jesus spoke to them at once and said, 'Courage, it is I; do not be afraid'. These words created peace in the hearts of the disciples and they realised that it was Jesus, the Son of God.

The above references, recorded during the time of Jesus' ministry with his disciples, present some of the reasons for claiming that Jesus is truly the Son of God. Through his Word, people today can become convinced that he is the Son of God. Christians today continue to believe in him as the Son of God, sent by God into the world to save the world from sin, and to give new life to people who believe in him.

Bibliography

Berkhof, Louis, *A Summary of Christian Doctrine*, Edinburgh: Eerdmans, 1939

Jesus as the High Chief

Peter Lai

Introduction

For me, Christ is the high chief in my society. He is the head man, with complete power and authority. He is the great helper, the head of the *nakamal*, the chief defender of our society, the occupant of the main house in the society and the person who provides total pastoral care.

The high chief

The birth of a high chief

In my own culture and tradition, whenever a high chief is born, the birth will always be accompanied by the blowing of the bubu shell. This is to announce to the people that the new and future high chief, who in time to come will assist his father, has been born. After the sounding of the bubu, the people come together and hold a great feast in the chief's compound. They celebrate on into the evening the new-born chief who has come into the world. In the same evening, during the feast, the name of the new-born high chief is announced. This name is given only to the chiefly line (blood-line); it is a special name and it is used to represent chiefly authority. In this way we recognise a high chief in our society.

Power and authority

The chief is the man who has power over all the people and everyone is under the authority of the chief. Whenever there is a problem to be solved, the chief is the one who makes the decisions about what has to happen or what to do in the situation. The will of the chief is carried out by the councillors of the community, or the people who are closest to the chief. The high chief is like a judge, in fact he acts as the traditional custom judge because he holds the power to rule over his people and to decide for them. So it is that in times of trouble, judgements are made by the high chief. If anyone disobeys a high chief's order, then the high chief has authority to deal with that person.

The great helper

We always look to the chief as a helper in time of need. If we need help in any way, if there is any sadness, if there is any trouble, then the chief is there to help. The chief helps the people when there is a shortage of food, and whenever there is any aspect of our traditional ceremonies that needs to be dealt with then the chief, as the man responsible for our culture and tradition, is there to help. This role of helping is represented in the special ranking given in the naming of the high chief, which I referred to above.

The head of the *nakamal*

In the *nakamal* (the chief's meeting place), the high chief has a special way of calling together his people at any time that he wants. This special way of calling his people is by *tam-tam* or bubu shell, or occasionally the chief will call people by name. In the *nakamal*, the chief has a small number of people whom he appoints to carry out his work and implement his decisions and commands. These men are in the free service of the chief, but the chief will pay them their wages in his own way and in his own time.

Defender of the society

Whenever there are problems of conflict threatening the society, then the high chief is the one who stands in the front line of his people to defend and to protect them from danger or injury. Because of this, the chief may sometimes be injured or killed for his people. But in the case of conflict, the role of the chief is to try and bring peace between two conflicting parties. In the case of reconciliation and compensation, the chief will often be the one who makes the peace payment; this will cost the chief an amount of money, kava, pigs, mats, and so on. In this way we think of our chief as a man of peace and love, one who pours cold water to cool down the people in troubled times, and puts out the fire of anger; this is the imagery that we use in our Tannese culture.

Occupant of the main house

As I have said above, the chief is the head of the *nakamal* and the *nakamal* is located in the centre of the community. The reason that the chief's house is in the centre of the community is so that the chief can observe all the events and activities of the village and keep an eye on what is happening among his people. The chief's house is also in the centre of the community because the people want the chief to be there; they are happy to know that he is nearby and watching over them. He also makes sure that the village is kept clean.

A person ready to be consulted

Once upon a time, perhaps ten years ago, we had a problem in my home. I went along to consult the chief at about one o'clock in the morning. The chief was very willing to see me; ready even at that hour of the night to listen to me and advise me. He came in response to help me the following morning. In our society the high chief is the one whom the people know is ready and willing to help at any time, to reach out for the needy people and come to their aid. The high chief is also the one who helps if any of his people go to prison or need any financial or material help. Back in 1984, when I was sentenced to eighteen months jail, the high chief actually paid out the fine for me and I was set free.

Jesus Christ as the high chief

The birth of Jesus

When we consider the birth of Jesus Christ, as told in the Gospels, we find that it is very similar to the birth of a high chief in our society. Jesus Christ is God himself who became incarnate and lived in this world with his people. Jesus also existed before the foundation of the world. This means that Jesus is the God-man (John 1:1–8, 3:13; Matthew 1:21–23). This illustrates the point that Jesus Christ is the head of all humanity, the high chief of both earth and heaven, the Saviour of the world who will save his people from their sin.

Power and authority

When we look at and compare the two powers and authorities (that is, of the cultural high chief of our society and that of Jesus), we can see that the power and authority of the high chief in our traditional culture is limited. However, despite its limitations, it is a good reflection of how Jesus ruled and worked as the God-man in the world during his lifetime two thousand years ago. In the great commission at the end of the Gospel of St Matthew, after the disciples have bowed down in worship of Jesus, Jesus says to them: 'All power and authority in heaven and on earth has been given to me' (Matthew 28:18–20). This power and this authority is eternal.

The great helper

In this role of our traditional high chief, he reflects very well the manner of Jesus' ministry upon the earth. Jesus responded to the needs of the poor and the sick, and provided for those even overcome by death (for example, Lazarus in John 11). Jesus is our great helper in everyday life, in a manner very similar to the high chief in our society.

The head of the church

The high chief is the head of the physical *nakamal*, but Jesus Christ is the head of the invisible church. We say that Jesus bought the church with his own blood on the cross. That is why we say that Christ is the head of the church and the head of everyone in the world today who believes in him as their Lord and Saviour.

The defender

When we compare the high priest and Jesus Christ, the high chief is a reflection of what Jesus Christ has promised to do in his power as defender in times of trouble. Christ is the true defender (Mark 16:18); he is amongst us as one who protects and defends (Luke 21:1–18; Revelation 7:1–17).

The centre of our society and life

The work of Jesus Christ puts him at the centre of our society. For Christians he is also the centre of their hearts. As the one who has come to seek out and to save the lost, Jesus becomes the centre of our lives. For Christians Jesus is the centre of all that they are and do, the centre of their lives and all that they own.

Christ the counsellor

Jesus said, 'Behold I stand at the door and knock' (Revelation 3:20). We have seen that the high chief is the man who is always ready at any time to help people in need. In this sense too, the high chief reflects Jesus Christ who is always there at the door of our hearts, waiting and ready to be our counsellor. I have spoken above about how the high chief is ready to be consulted at any time by one of his people, take him or her into his care, to free them from the punishment that is theirs and to help in solving their problems. This is a very good reflection of the role of Jesus Christ as counsellor. On the cross Jesus took our sins, suffered for us and died to save us from eternal death. In response we offer ourselves to him in our daily life.

Conclusion

The best way to conclude is to quote from Isaiah 9:6–7:

> For to us a child is born, to us a son is given; and the government will be upon his shoulders. And he will be called Wonderful Counsellor, Mighty God, Everlasting Father, Prince of Peace. Of the increase of his government there will be no end. He will reign on David's throne and over his Kingdom, establishing and upholding it with justice and righteousness from that time on and forevermore. The zeal of the Lord of hosts will accomplish this.

Jesus as the Chief

Kalmatak Ian Tino Sope

A long time ago, in the times of darkness, before the missionaries arrived in our country with the good news of Jesus Christ, our chiefs were the rulers around our villages and islands, from the north to the south of the country. The chief had a very important role to play. His responsibility was to take care of his people during good times and bad times. In this essay I will carefully discuss some of the very important roles and activities of the chief and indicate in what ways the chief cared for the people of his village. I will then show that the chief is a valuable image in our understanding of Jesus Christ, especially in four ways:

1. The chief is appointed by God to lead his people.
2. The chief knows all the custom medicine leaves and practices to cure every sickness.
3. The chief is always ready to help his people in times of need.
4. The chief is always ready to fight to defend his people, even to die for them.

The chief appointed by God

In the days of our ancestors, the traditional role of the chief was to be a leader for his people. This involved protecting the people from danger, keeping the peace, and if there was trouble or warfare, seeking ways to establish the peace again. The chief was responsible for maintaining the harmony of the village and to ensure that his people lived a happy life. The chief had to hold the respect of his people and maintain that respect.

The wisdom and skill to carry out these roles did not come from a good education, but came from God. It was from God that the traditional rules and ways of our culture came, and it was from God that the chief was given the authority and wisdom to rule his people, to protect the community, to safeguard the cultural life, and to ensure obedience to the village rules.

When the missionaries came to our country in the nineteenth century they learned to respect the chiefs, their wisdom and the rules that they upheld. The missionaries also realised just how much respect the people had for their chief; when the chief spoke, the people obeyed. It was the chief who ruled the people and it was to him that the people looked for advice. The chief was like a first-born brother to all his people, leading his people with wisdom and care, in the way that God enabled him.

The chiefs and custom medicine for healing sickness

One of the important skills and responsibilities of the chief in our culture is to do with custom medicine. The chief knows all the custom medicines and the leaves that can cure the sicknesses of his people. Sometimes the chief would learn the right leaf to use by God showing it to him in a dream. The leaves grow on local plants that are all around us. God instructed the chiefs in all sorts of ways, even through the traditional worship of stones or snakes. It is only the chiefs and no ordinary person who has the custom rights to use these medicines. Since the arrival of the missionaries, there are other ways of curing sickness that have also come from God, and this knowledge has been given to other people.

The chief who is always ready to help

The chief is like a father to all his people, and also to strangers who may happen to travel through or come into his village. Daytime or night-time, the chief is ready to offer a welcome to his people. If people are in great need, they will always look to their leaders to help them. In many of our villages, chiefs build their *nakamal* (chief's meeting house) in the middle of their village, in order to accommodate the people who are in need. The chief's *nakamal* is a meeting place where many people come together regularly (such as once a week) to listen to their leader.

If the chief has an important message for his people, or if the people are fighting between each other over various issues and problems (for example, land disputes, boundaries, conflict between church groups or clans or tribes, or disputes over ranking titles given by the ancestors), the only way of resolving the problems is to sit down in the *nakamal* and allow the chief to sort it out and decide on the way of peace.

The chief will always make sure that the people are ruled with justice; he will judge their cases carefully through the knowledge and the wisdom that God has given him. He listens to every case and must recognise the rights of his people. The custom laws that guide the chief in finding right and just solutions to the problems in the village come from God, and are given in order that the people might live in harmony and have respect and honour towards their leader. In times of trouble, the people will always look to their leader for help.

The chief – always ready to fight, or even die, for his people

In the 'heathen' times before the gospel came, the chiefs led their people to war against other chiefs. The chief would always advise his people about how to fight against their enemies. In time of war the chief was the leader standing in the front, the one to give the orders, and the one who would even be prepared to die for his people. In everything, including in times of warfare, the chief was like a first-born brother or a father to his people.

Jesus – the first-born brother according to the gospel

1. Jesus is chosen and appointed by God

In the gospel, we read about God's only Son Jesus Christ, who is the Saviour of the world. He was God himself and he was the eternal Word (John 1:1–5). It was Jesus whom God chose and appointed to be the leader of God's chosen people.

2. Jesus has power to heal and to cure sickness

When Jesus Christ lived in the world as a man, he travelled through many places, teaching the people and healing their sicknesses. He performed many miracles and did great wonders in the eyes of the people, proving to them that he was the Son of God, the Messiah, the one promised through the prophets from long ago.

3. Jesus is ready to help his people in times of need

When Jesus Christ lived his life in the world, he understood the needs of the people and had compassion upon them in times of trouble. At the wedding at Cana, Jesus responded to the needs of the people by turning water into wine (John 2:1–11). When Jesus raised the widow's son from death, we see again how Jesus shows his love and is ready to help people when they are in great need (Luke 7:11–17).

4. Jesus is ready to die for his people

We are sinners, born into a world of sin, but because of God's love towards us, he gave his only Son to die for us on the cross and to save us from the power of Satan and sin (John 3:16). Because of Jesus' death and resurrection, we have been given new life in God through faith in his Son. He will continue to be with us until the end of the age (Matthew 28:20).

Conclusion

By exploring the understanding of the chief in our traditional culture, I have used a symbolic way of relating the gospel to our culture and relating our culture to the gospel. The chief is like a first-born brother, a father, who is also a leader, ready to help his people. It is the same with Jesus Christ, the only Son of God. He is like our first-born brother who died for us two thousand years ago, setting us free from sin. Even today, this same Jesus is always ready to help us in times of trouble and need, physically and spiritually.

Jesus Our Uncle

Urick Lui

We can claim, from our cultural point of view, that Jesus is our uncle because we can see that the responsibilities of an uncle in our culture are the same as the responsibilities that Jesus exercises for all people. Let me make clear what I am saying in using this title, 'Jesus our Uncle'.

Uncle (or *Tarabe*)

In the dictionary, 'uncle' means the brother of one's father or mother, or the husband of one's aunt. But in our culture, on the northern part of Pentecost Island, 'uncle' or *Tarabe* refers to the brother of one's mother. It is he who is the one leading man in the family line or tribe.

The responsibilities of an uncle

The first responsibility for an uncle is to provide for his family line or tribal ground. He must ensure that every member of his line or tribe has enough ground on which to grow their food. If one of his tribe is in need of land for a garden or a business, then they must seek the advice of the uncle and gain his permission to use the ground.

Secondly, the uncle is the one to organise the payment of the bride-price for all the males in his family line. During the period of preparation for marriage and during the marriage itself, the uncle is the one who is responsible for the provision of mats, food, firewood, water, money and so on.

A third responsibility for the uncle is to be the leader of his family line in decision-making and in resolving problems. He is the one who is consulted in all family matters. For example, if a fight breaks out with another family, then the uncle will be the first one to stand on the frontline. He is the peace-maker when there is a tribal war. In some cases he will be the one to die for the sake of his family.

When there is conflict involving a family member, or when a family member has done something wrong against another person, it is the uncle who is responsible for compensation and provides the red mat, the pig, money, or whatever is needed, for the family who have been wronged.

On an occasion of death (for example, when a man dies who has married a sister of an uncle or brother), the uncle is responsible for oversight of all that needs to happen after the death. This includes the ceremonial arrangements for the family and the provision of food. Everything that the family owns is under his care.

The uncle is the one to whom the family goes for all sorts of small matters. For example, when someone wants some particular physical help, they will go to the uncle and the uncle is obliged to help them. Whether in good times or bad times the uncle is expected to do this. He is the one who provides the material help for all the family.

Status of an uncle

The uncle is the man who does the collective thinking for his family line and he carries the concern for all his people. An uncle is a chief to all the members of his family line.

This is the process by which an uncle comes to the rank of being the chief. He must go through a series of steps until he reaches the highest rank of a chiefly position. The second-last rank in our community is called *Vira* and the last is called *Tugoro*. In order to go through all of these ranking steps, all members of his family line must support him with pigs, food, red mats, and so on. They must be prepared to offer this support because he is the head of their line, and they look to him as their chief, their leader and the man of high rank in the family. Through him, all members of the family line will prosper.

Christ and the tribal uncle

In the same way that an uncle provides for his family, for example, with enough ground for their gardens, so Jesus is the one who provides for his people. Whenever we ask for anything in prayer, it is given. In John 14:13–14, Jesus promises to do whatever we ask in his name, and again in John 15:16, we are told that God the Father will give anything that we ask in Jesus' name.

In the same way that an uncle responds to the particular needs of his family line, so also Jesus is the one who provides for our needs. In John 10:9, we are told that Jesus is 'the gate' for the sheep and whoever enters through him will be saved. Through Jesus we enter into the sheepfold and find pasture. In other words, all of our needs are met by Jesus and we can go to him with any request.

Just as an uncle is the leading man in the family line – the one who stands at the front when his family are under threat from another family or tribe, and the one who will even die for his family – is also this is true of Jesus. In John 10:11 Jesus says, 'I am the good shepherd. The good shepherd lays down his life for the sheep.' Jesus expresses the fact that he is ready to die for our sake because we are his people.

In the description above I have explained how an uncle is responsible for the family of his brother-in-law (that is, the family of his sister's husband). This responsibility to care for and to provide for the family is exercised in many ways, for example, on the occasion of the death of a family member, as I have described. In a similar way, Jesus takes responsibility for our lives. In Matthew 10:17–20, Jesus sends out his twelve disciples and says to them, 'Be aware of people. They will arrest you and take you to court to charge you, but do not be afraid because I will tell you what you are to say.'

When a member of the family creates trouble with another family, there is a process in which the uncle resolves the problem and brings peace. He does this on behalf of the member of his own family through offering a gift, such as a red mat or a pig, to the family who has been wronged. When Jesus prays to his Father, as recorded in John 17:12, he includes this prayer for his disciples: 'While I was with them, I protected them and kept them safe ...' In other words, Jesus, as our uncle, helps us in our times of trouble.

An uncle has the role of providing all the general needs of his family if and when they ask him. He is obliged to do this whether in good times or in bad times. There are many examples in Jesus' life where he shows that he is ready to help the people who come to him. In John 17:20–24 the prayer of Jesus includes a prayer for his community of disciples and for all who will come to believe in him in the future. Jesus knows that he is going to die on the cross and so prays for all his disciples and those who will believe in him. He is wanting to prepare them for both good and bad times in the future, and to make everything ready for them after his death on the cross. In John 14:20 Jesus says to his disciples, 'Whoever has my commands and obeys them is the one who loves me. He who loves me will be loved by my Father and I too will love him and show myself to him.'

Conclusion

I have set out the close relationship between the role of an uncle in our traditional culture and the role that Jesus plays in the lives of his people. In fact, the roles are so similar that it is possible to speak of Jesus as 'our uncle'. This has great meaning to the people of our Vanuatu cultures.

Dolphins Reflecting Jesus Christ

Sheila Yamsiu

Introduction

Dolphins are very intelligent and lively creatures of the sea. They are playful and a wonderful sight to observe. Sometimes, if you go down to the beach and are very lucky, you can see a school of them swimming in the sea nearby. Dolphins are well known around the world and are famous for the many stories told about them. They are often friendly to human beings and very gentle towards them; dolphins have saved human lives.

In some of the cultures around Vanuatu, dolphins were regarded by the ancestors as the gods and protectors of the sea. Dolphins have existed in my own culture from the very beginning and, from my own understanding, the dolphin is a traditional cultural god for my people. If you study a dolphin closely, observing its characteristics, you will be able to see why the dolphin is a good reflection of the significance of Jesus Christ. In this paper I will speak of just three of their many characteristics and indicate how they reflect Jesus Christ as Saviour and Shepherd.

Characteristics of the dolphin in relation to Jesus Christ

1. Dolphins like to swim in seas that are rough or choppy, rather than in the calm waters or lagoons, and so it is in the rough or choppy weather conditions that you are more likely to see them. Occasionally dolphins may come into the lagoons, but they cannot stay for long – they have to return to the ocean. I am not sure why they have this preference for rough conditions, perhaps because it is more fun for them to play in them.

Jesus Christ our Saviour came into the world not to be among the righteous people, but to be among the unrighteous, the sinner. Jesus' preference was for these 'rough seas' rather than the 'calm or smooth seas'. In that sense there is a connection with the dolphins. Jesus did not carry out his ministry in the company of the Pharisees and teachers of the law, but in the company of the tax-collectors, the fishermen, the sinners, the outcasts, the unlawful people, and it was from among these that he chose his disciples. He came into the world to seek and save the sinners, not the righteous (Matthew 9:13).

2. Dolphins have shown themselves to be the friends of human beings. They attack sharks, which are a dangerous enemy to humans and of which human beings are afraid. If dolphins are able to attack and kill sharks, it suggests that they are stronger than sharks. Some people have told of being saved from sharks by dolphins while swimming in the ocean. My understanding is that if a human being is swimming in the midst of a school of dolphins and a shark comes along, then the human being will be quite safe within the boundaries of the dolphins; the shark will be too afraid to make an attack on the human.

Dolphins display a manner that is friendly, caring and protective towards humans and are quite capable of saving them from the enemy shark.

So it is with Jesus Christ. Jesus came into the world to save us from the biggest of all our enemies – Satan. He came as a human, he suffered as a human, he died on the cross at Calvary, his precious blood flowed and he cleansed us from our sins. He was raised on the third day and ascended into heaven to be with the Father. Jesus Christ is the only one who can save us from our transgressions and give us everlasting peace, joy and love. If we live 'within the boundaries' of Jesus Christ, that is, if we put ourselves in the loving arms of Jesus' presence by believing in him, in his death and resurrection, then the enemy Satan is not able to attack us because Jesus has more power than Satan. The image of the dolphin is able to help us to better understand that Jesus is our Saviour.

3. Dolphins always swim in front of a ship or boat when it is going in and out of the harbour. This is well known by those who watch dolphins carefully. It is as if the dolphins are guiding the ship safely into the harbour and out again. This gives the impression in my culture that the dolphin is protecting the ship as it goes out to sea and welcoming it back when it returns to harbour. In the past, if my ancestors saw a ship coming to their island and it was being led by dolphins, then they knew that the ship was coming with friendly people on board, and so they accepted the ship into their harbour and the passengers onto their island.

This behaviour of the dolphins suggests the image of Jesus as the good shepherd (John 10). Jesus is the shepherd who guides us to a way of peace, joy and eternal life. He guides us safely into the loving arms of God, into God's presence, making the relationship between humans and God right again, after the fall of humankind (recorded in Genesis 2 and 3). Jesus guides us cheerfully, lovingly, joyfully, peacefully into God's presence. Every day, in our spiritual life, it is Jesus Christ who leads us as a shepherd. It is this Jesus to whom we must look and who we must follow, just as a sheep follows a shepherd, as a ship follows behind a dolphin.

Conclusion

There are many things from our culture that we might choose as good symbols that reflect Jesus Christ for us. Our ancestors, before the arrival of the missionaries, worshipped such things with great respect and great faith. It was because they were people of such respect and faith that when the missionaries came, it was easy for the missionaries to develop an understanding of our gods, and for our ancestors to develop an understanding of the Christian God.

Dolphins are one of those ancient gods. They really reflect Jesus Christ in their characteristics, and Jesus Christ is really like a dolphin in his characteristics – gentle, caring, friendly. In this way it is easy for me to see Jesus in our traditional culture and to appreciate the strong links between out traditional culture and the gospel of Jesus Christ.

Jesus and the Dolphin

Martin Namel

This paper explores the question of how we might understand Jesus Christ within our culture and how it is possible to understand who Jesus is through observing the behaviour of some of the living things in our culture. In this way we can make a symbolic connection between Jesus and our culture. In my own culture it is the symbol of the dolphin that I want to use to represent the relationship between Jesus Christ and culture. There are many aspects of the dolphin that point to the character of Jesus Christ. Of course the dolphin is not the only living creature that may be able to symbolise Jesus Christ. It is possible that all living creatures could be used as symbols of Christ in some way. I am choosing the dolphin because it is an important part of my own culture.

The dolphin

The dolphin is not a fish but a mammal that lives in the sea. It can be quite big and has the shape of most large fish. Its life setting is the sea and it is in the sea that it displays its nature, which seems more advanced than many other creatures. How does a dolphin and its nature point us to Jesus Christ?

Love

The dolphin displayed love to our forefathers when in their canoes they found themselves drifting away from the shoreline. The dolphin would swim up to the canoe, sometimes just one of them, and sometimes in a school of five to ten. They come, not to attack the people in the canoe but to be friendly and to keep them company, as if out of love for the people. They show this apparent love by entertaining the people in the canoe, jumping and shaking their tails on the surface of the sea. This attracts the attention of the people in the canoe. In this sense, the dolphin is like Jesus Christ. Christ comes to people, not to attack but to show his love. He does not come to accuse them nor to be angry towards them as people who have done something wrong, but to love and forgive them (John 15:9; Mark 10:21; Matthew 11:5).

Comfort

In our local community on the coast of the island of Erromango, when people who are out in their canoes want to return to the shore, and the waters are not clear so that they cannot easily find their way, a dolphin comes to them and guides them through the waters back to the shore. The dolphins lead the people in the canoe on the very route that the people need to go to reach the shore safely, and then they return to the deeper waters at the end of the reef. The dolphin is of great help and comfort to the people in the canoe. In the same way, Jesus Christ is our helper and our comforter (2 Corinthians 1:5–6). He helps the people who are in need, he heals people, he feeds the people, he blesses the people. As comforter and helper in times of trouble, Jesus Christ is like the dolphin.

Protection

In my culture, the ancestors and forefathers know the dolphin as a protector who guards them from the dangerous creatures of the sea. The most dangerous sea creature for my people is the shark. There is always danger of a shark attack, but a shark will never attack a person if a dolphin is near. There is a story told of one of my ancestors who was out on a canoe when it turned over and sank. He was in danger, but a school of dolphins came and swam around him until he was rescued. In a similar way, Jesus Christ is our protector (John 17:12); he protects his people and saves them from evil; he has come to save his people and guard them from the enemy (see, for example, the exorcism story in Mark 5:1–20).

Humility

Dolphins seem to be very humble creatures. Even if they have been harmed by people, they never take revenge. They seem to humble themselves in all their behaviour with people. We can reflect on this behaviour as we think about Jesus Christ who died on a cross to save us. Even though we caused him pain and suffering, he humbled himself, even through great difficulties, and in the end he died on the cross for us (Philippians 2:8).

Conclusion

However we may understand Jesus Christ in relation to culture, it is helpful in my culture to speak of Jesus Christ using the symbol of the dolphin. I have shown some of the characteristics of the dolphin and how the dolphin shows us some things about Jesus Christ. In this way we can learn about Jesus Christ through important cultural symbols.

Jesus and the Octopus

Worai Kalsakau

Introduction

In this paper I am writing about the relationship between my own culture and the Christian gospel, and how there may be aspects of my culture that help us to understand that gospel. I want to focus on the octopus, which is one of the clan names in my culture.

The octopus is a living creature of the sea. In our language we call it *'wita'* or 'black *wita'*. There are several kinds of octopus living in our area (for example, another is named 'one-hand octopus'). The cultures of the people on the island of Efate commonly use such familiar creatures as family clan names and people then identify their ancestors by using this clan name. These clan names include also yam, coconut, and many others.

The octopus as guardian

Of all the different clan names, the most important one among our people is the octopus. The octopus is the clan name of the head of the village, the one who holds the responsibilities of chief of the people. We believe that our ancient gods gave to us the octopus to be the head, the guardian. We have a special place where the octopus lives – it is situated at the main wharf where the ships anchor when they come in.

Why is the octopus clan important?

The importance of the octopus is that many centuries ago a great chief, Roimata, gave the names of the clans to the people, to help them identify their own ancestors. Within my own community, the octopus is identified with the leadership clan; it is the clan that is the biggest and fastest growing. The people of this clan have their own *nasara* (meeting house) and their own council, led by a chief who controls the clan. All of the village communities and cultures around Efate operate with this same sort of governing system, which has come from Roimata.

If an octopus is killed by a person ...

The octopus can be a friend as well as an enemy. If a person kills or destroys an octopus, my people believe that the guilty person will be cursed by the octopus and their life will be destroyed. This is the power of the octopus. Long ago, the people were afraid to walk by themselves near where the wharf is now, where the octopus live. If today you visit the wharf, there is a paw-paw tree in the shape of an octopus. Some years ago, a group of people cut down the paw-paw and as a result they became very sick and nearly died. They realised that they had done something wrong and a special custom ceremony was held by the chief to cure them. They recovered their health.

The octopus and Jesus Christ

Today our people think that the octopus and its powers was created by God and given to the people. It is a good symbol for Jesus Christ in the sense that the octopus was a guardian for the people, a provider of food, a protector from harm, and sustainer of good leadership, maintaining peace and harmony in the village.

Although the octopus is a good symbol for Jesus Christ, in fact the significance of Jesus is much greater than the octopus can symbolise. Jesus Christ came into the world as a man, he talked, walked, performed miracles, and in the end died on the cross for the sins of the world, according to the plan of God (see, for example, Romans 5:25).

Christ has more power than the power of creatures around us. God is the head of all things. God is omnipotent (that is, all powerful – see Isaiah 40:10ff), God is omnipresent (that is, present everywhere – see Psalm 139:7–8), and, unlike creatures, God does not change (see Malachi 3:6; James 1:17). Creatures like the octopus may be able to be symbols of Jesus Christ, but as symbols they are very limited because Jesus Christ has done more than any of these things can symbolise.

How do I understand Jesus Christ in my culture?

In my view, Jesus Christ is best understood as provider, life-giver, lighthouse, ship's captain, to name a few things. I understand that there is a close connection between my culture and God because God created all things and created humankind in God's own image, with different powers and responsibilities – moral, social and spiritual (Genesis 1:26–28). There are also demonic spirits that surround us and threaten us.

I understand that in Jesus Christ, God has come to us and died for our sins so that we are clean enough to approach our holy God. Our cultures can contribute to the breakdown of our relationship with God and our relationship with each other, and can damage our relationship with Jesus Christ. Creation is under the responsibility of humans and we can use it in proper ways or improper ways. People can be careless in the way culture is used by destroying our being in the image of God. There is good and there is evil in human life and in culture, and it is possible for people to use culture to destroy each other. Christ has come not to destroy but to give life.

Conclusion

It is my belief that Jesus Christ is the head of all things on earth and in heaven; through his death and resurrection, this authority was given to him by God.

The well-known theologian C. H. Spurgeon put it in this way:

> Nothing will so enlarge the intellect, nothing so magnify the whole soul of man, as a devout, earnest, continued investigation of the great subject of the Deity. Would you lose your sorrow? Would you drown your cares? Then go, plunge yourself in the Godhead's deepest sea, be lost in his immensity and you shall come forth as from a couch of rest, refreshed and invigorated. I know nothing which can so comfort the soul, so calm the swelling billows of sorrow and grief, so speak peace to the wind of trial, as a devout musing upon the subject of the Godhead. (Quoted in Peter Jeffery, *Christian Handbook*, Wales: Bryntirion Press, 2000)

Jesus Christ and Pig-killing

Simeon Tavui

Introduction

The people of my community understand their culture very well, but they would never think that there might be anything within their culture that might help them to understand Jesus Christ, or that might be a sign of the Christian gospel. They just think of the culture as culture.

In this paper I will be considering a symbol that I think is the best one in our culture as a symbol for Jesus Christ. It is the symbol of the killing of pigs, which in my culture is a very important practice and is clearly understood. As I consider this symbol, I will be looking at two aspects: the kind of pigs used and the actual role of pig-killing. After looking at these two aspects I will then indicate how we might speak of Jesus Christ in the terms of pig-killing, and finally I will draw some conclusions.

The kind of pigs

Some generations ago, my ancestors used various things to solve their problems, for example, mats or chickens. But these things are not deeply rooted in our culture; they just used them as a way of expressing a thank-you or making a gesture. The thing that is firmly rooted in our culture, however, is the pig; it is the pig that has been part of our culture throughout our long past, right up until the present. There is nothing that is more deeply rooted in our culture than the pig.

Pigs are used on most feast occasions. For example, pigs are always used for marriage ceremonies, for chiefly ceremonies, for burial ceremonies. This does not mean that any kind of pig will be satisfactory because in fact, especially since the missionaries came with the Christian gospel, only certain kinds of pigs are acceptable. Female pigs, for example, cannot be used. The pigs that are used are male pigs, especially those that are castrated and have grown a large tusk. If a pig is going to be used for a ceremony, that pig must also be a healthy pig without any problems or without anything abnormal about its body.

(The reason why female pigs are no longer good for ceremonial use is because our Christian forefathers told us that Christ is not a

61

woman but a man, and the pig must therefore be male. The reason why an unhealthy pig or a pig with any marks or spots is not used is because Christ was righteous and without spot or stain.)

The role of pig-killing in culture

Throughout the generations the pig has been a highly respected animal. In fact, the pig has an important place in all cultures of the people of Vanuatu. On major occasions, for example, marriages and resolving disputes between two parties, pig-killing has a central part to play.

The first thing that is important is the blood of the pig. Blood symbolises life and it is through the blood of the pig that, for example, peace is brought to two fighting parties. Secondly, the pig can have the role of being a sacrificial animal. If a person of one tribe murders a person from another tribe, then instead of the murderer being put to death, a pig will be killed as a substitute. The spilling of the blood of the pig brings peace. The presence of the blood from the pig, running out from the pig's body, represents the spilling out of all the dispute and anger, leaving the people to live in peace.

Christ and pig-killing in our culture

There are many people who oppose the idea of speaking of Jesus Christ in terms of pig-killing in our culture. It has caused argument. But if we look very closely at the meaning of pig-killing and think carefully about Jesus Christ, we see that pig-killing is a helpful symbol. Jesus came into the world, was born as a child in a manger and grew up; through his ministry many people opposed him and argued with him until in the end he was put to death on a cross. He was a righteous man who had done nothing wrong to deserve death. He humbled himself to death on the cross. His death is very important to us as Christians because although we have done many wrong things in our life, we do not die for our sins. Jesus Christ died for our transgressions and he replaced us. And the blood of Jesus Christ is important because through the blood of Jesus we are cleansed from sin.

Therefore pigs and the blood of pigs are a very valuable symbol in understanding Jesus Christ. Pigs are born in muddy enclosures or in the bushes; we care for them and when it is time for the solving of problems, we take them and kill them. Fighting, rape or any dispute, is solved through the killing of the pig. Through the blood of the pig we have peace with others and stability in the community. The pig replaces us in our wrong doings, so that we might be free and not be put to death.

The pig is represented in the flag of Vanuatu with its tusks. The

Christian faith is represented on the flag in the colour yellow. Thus on the flag both gospel and culture are represented together. They must always go together.

Conclusion

It is very important for all people of all cultures to be able to relate their culture to the gospel of Jesus Christ. If we are not able to do that, we will be very unbalanced in both our culture and in the gospel. The combination of gospel and culture is represented in the national flag of Vanuatu and it needs to be taken seriously in the church.

As Christian people we must be very careful to understand the gospel within our culture in a right manner. To illustrate this I have chosen to represent the gospel of Jesus Christ in terms of pig-killing because the pig is so important in our cultural life, and the blood of the pig has an important and powerful part to play.

Jesus and the Canoe

Wilson Billy

Introduction

In the past, the canoe was the only form of transport that my people on Lelepa Island could use. This meant that the canoe was very important for us. The canoe is made from a strong and large tree that we find in the bush. The tree first needs to be cut down, then the canoe needs to be carved. It takes a lot of time and energy to complete the work. There are three main parts to the canoe: the main body, the outrigger, and the construction of timber and rope that joins and holds the canoe together.

The main body

On our home island, the first step in building a canoe is to find and then cut down the tree it will be made from. After we finish cutting the tree down in the bush, we ask people to help us transport it so that we can then cut out the main body for the canoe. It takes one or two days to complete the work. There is always one person who is in charge of the project of building.

The outrigger

The outrigger is the second main part of the canoe. When the first part has been completed, the carver then works on this second part; without the outrigger the canoe can never be used. But even with the outrigger to go with the main body, the canoe is still not complete.

The timber

The final part of the canoe is the collection of wooden pieces that go across from the main body to the outrigger. Rope is used for the binding of these pieces of wood. This third part of the canoe is as important as parts one and two.

As I stated above, the canoe is an important part of our cultural life. It costs us nothing to make and nothing to use. It serves us for transport; we can travel as far as we want in a canoe. The canoe also acts as a protector while we are at sea – we are only in danger if we fall out of the canoe. A canoe is also used for carrying our food and water, or anything that is heavy.

Relating the culture and the gospel

It is possible to understand the three parts of the canoe as God the Father, the Son and the Holy Spirit. They are three and one (Acts 10:38). God the Father anointed Jesus the Son with the Holy Spirit. Although there are three persons, they are one God. The gospel tells us that God gives us freedom through Jesus Christ and power through the Holy Spirit. Christ died on the cross to free us from our sins; we have the free gift of eternal life through Jesus Christ (Romans 6:23).

God cares for us and saves us in times of trouble. He does this through the blood of his Son Jesus; we are saved by grace (Ephesians 2:5). Only God can lift our burdens from us when we are carrying a heavy load:

> Come to me, all you who are weary and are carrying heavy burdens, and I will give you rest. Take my yoke upon you, and learn from me; for I am gentle and humble in heart, and you will find rest for your souls. For my yoke is easy, and my burden is light. (Matthew 11:28–30)

Conclusion

As the canoe helps us in so many ways in our culture, so Jesus Christ is our help in so many ways in our life. By dying on the cross for our sins, he shows us his love. While the canoe has its own value in our culture, it is also valuable in pointing us to Jesus Christ.

Life's Origin

Gideon Paul

Culture is about a way of life – the way people believe, the way people worship, the way people govern themselves, the way people relate to each other. Therefore when we talk about 'life origin', we are talking about the way our ancestors came to be and how they existed on these islands.

It must be understood that in Vanuatu we have different cultures and within the different cultures we have different creation stories about our beginnings. When the question is asked, Where did you come from? or What was your origin?, the answer will always be something like: We came from a *shark*, or an *octopus*, or a *yam*, or a *snake*. Any such thing may be mentioned.

Culturally, each person or tribe knows the formation story of their own beginning that has been passed down through the generations orally. How things began, the earliest existence of humans, how man got a partner, how they began to live together and have children, and so on – all these things are traditional stories in our culture that were credible to our ancestors and were passed on.

Even today in some places, some of these stories are understood to be true and accurate practical accounts. For example, those who come from the octopus actually treat the octopus in the sea differently from all other sea creatures. For example, they may not eat octopus or kill octopus. In the same way, those who come from the yam will treat yam differently from other root crops. The reason for this is that people have a special respect for their culturally understood origins. They also have certain regulations and beliefs about what they must do and believe in order to be successful in life; these regulations must be kept. Our ancestors believed that if someone within the tribe is sick or facing some kind of disaster, then this means that he or she done something wrong. Some kind of sacrifice must be made to their ancestral origin so that their life and fortune is restored and they can again be prosperous with their gardening, poultry, pigs and so on.

In relation to Christology

According to the accounts of creation in the Old Testament book of Genesis, we were created in the image of God. With this account and with our own tradition, we are pulled into two extremes, the cultural and the biblical understandings of our beginnings. As Christians we are to accept the Genesis account that in fact we are created by God, but it is also important to keep the cultural understanding of our beginnings because that is how our ancestors thought. Although they did not know God as Creator, they did have their own belief in creation.

When we think about the biblical story of creation and the origins of life, we can identify some biblical insights about Christology. When Jesus Christ was incarnate in this world, people thought that he was born to a human father, Joseph the carpenter; however he was the Son of God. Later in his ministry he taught the people that he was the Son of God, confirming the angel's message to Mary at the time of his birth (Luke 1:26–38).

Our cultural understanding of the creation stories has followed a similar pattern. From the beginning our ancestors thought of their origins in terms of an octopus, or shark, or yam, et cetera, but in later generations it was known that God is Creator, giver of life, the one who alone is to be worshipped.

Secondly, Christ is always to be worshipped as Son of God – at one time he physically dwelt with us, suffered, died, was buried and was raised from the dead and sent us his Holy Spirit. Our worship to God is offered through his name; he is provider and forgiver of sins.

According to our ancestors, their gods who had, they believed, given them life were to be highly respected. Our ancestors believed that it was their gods who provided their needs, and so various regulations were important to keep in order for the continuity of life to be preserved. Anyone who broke any of the regulations needed to offer some kind of sacrifice to their god; otherwise the blessings of life would be taken away from them.

There are other things that could be said about relating together the two origin stories: the cultural one and the Genesis one. For example, there are some connections about healing and communication. Our ancestors had their own way of approaching their gods for healing and their own way of communicating with their gods. This is how we now understand Christ in our context, as healer and as the one through whom we communicate with God.

When we look back to our cultural way of life, and how our ancestors believed, how they worshiped, how they related to one another, how they understood their origins, there are close connections with the Genesis story. In this way we could say that Christ was already with our ancestors but they did not know him. Later, in the sharing of the gospel, our ancestors came to know the one who is their true creator, namely God the Father Almighty. They were converted and their beliefs changed from belief in the worldly gods to belief in the living God.

Part Two

Mission

The Challenge of Mission to the Presbyterian Church of Vanuatu

Pastor Shem Tamara

Introduction

Mission has not been effectively carried out by the Presbyterian Church of Vanuatu (PCV) since the days of the pioneer missionaries. The issue came to life again in the 1997 PCV annual general assembly when the theme of Bible study was missions. The leaders of the church around the islands who attended the Bible study were challenged to think seriously about mission, even during the group discussions. I was also challenged myself.

When we talk about missions, people often think of people who go out to another country to share the good news of Jesus Christ. Many people in the PCV would think that if God has not called them to go to another country then they do not have a part to play in mission. In other words, mission is only for those who go to foreign or distant lands. I would like to challenge this way of thinking in the PCV. Mission work should involve every Christian member of the church. I want to speak of mission in the following four categories: the areas of knowing, praying, giving and going.

Knowing

The PCV has come to realise that the failure to be effectively involved in missions is due to the failure of any teaching about missions. The church took the initiative to start a mission course in 1999. It is good to see men and women who are enthusiastic about missions and who seek to train for it. But I think the backbone of missions is the local church. The students who do the teaching course become trained and they will be available to be missionaries. But who is going to support them? The pastor is there, maybe the mission committee, but they have no idea of what to do. Mission education needs to take place across the whole church in order to grow 'World Christians'. This involves three things: understanding of the Word, understanding the world, and understanding the church's role.

Understanding of the Word

The biblical basis for missions is the starting point for educating the church about missions. The concern for missions must flow out of the conviction that Scripture mandates it and that the church exists to be a missionary church. The PCV needs to learn that identifying, preparing and sending missionaries is the norm for a local church (Pollard, pp. 84–5).

Understanding the world

For the PCV to become effective in mission the members need to know what is happening in the world. (See 'Work of a mission mobiliser' below for more details.)

Understanding the church's role

The people in the PCV should know those who are PCV missionaries in Vanuatu and overseas. The church needs to understand that missions are not only what is done 'over there', but something in which every Christian has a part to play. I believe the PCV needs a 'mission mobiliser'.

Work of a mission mobiliser

The work of a mission mobiliser would be:
- to increase the interest of the church in mission,
- to regularly pass on information and prayer topics to the churches,
- to encourage local churches to have a regular mission segment during church services,
- to let the church know when there are special mission awareness and training meetings available,
- to arrange for the church to have a yearly or half yearly mission weekend or conference,
- to keep up to date with what is happening in those parts of the world that the church is especially interested in,
- to arrange and lead prayer meetings for missions,
- to pass out letters and mission news,
- to organise prayer for mission in various church groups,
- to make a mission display board and place it where all can see it,
- to use photographs and maps showing where overseas missionaries are and where there are opportunities to go overseas as a missionary,
- to encourage the pastors and lay preachers to preach about missions, and
- to look for new ways to get people involved with missions.

Teaching of PCV church history

The lecturer for church history at Talua should not only teach students about history but should always challenge them about what can be done for missions today.

Commemoration Day

For years the PCV has been celebrating the arrival of missionaries who came to different islands around Vanuatu. I think the PCV should not only remember their history but should organise with a missions mobiliser to have some teaching on mission or a mission conference. Instead of just a 'remembrance' day it can also become a 'missions' day. In some local churches they could have two to three days of celebration. Funds could be raised towards those days. I believe that funds that people spend for food and drink should be used for mission work.

PCV Missionary Sunday

I wonder how many pastors preach about missions on this special annual Sunday that is part of the PCV annual calendar. Missionary Sunday does not mean anything to the church members. This is because nothing is said about mission work. I cannot remember a Missionary Sunday during which someone talked about mission work. The only thing I can remember is the announcement, 'Today is Missionary Sunday, all our tithes and offerings will go towards missionaries.' The PCV should make this Sunday more meaningful to the congregations. There could be a weekend teaching on missions. There should be a mission spot in worship, and the preaching should be on missions.

Missionary work in and out of Vanuatu

In the PCV, we have missionaries who are working in Vanuatu – both locals and expatriates – and we also have PCV missionaries overseas. As far as I understand the congregations do not know about these missionaries. They might have heard that a missionary is in Australia or New Caledonia, but that is all. These missionaries should be made known to the local churches. They should also be allowed to speak in different churches about their work in missions. This will help the congregations to know them and pray for them, or even to support them financially.

Praying

Christians are commanded by our Lord to pray for mission fields. Prayer should not be seen simply as a supportive work for mission – prayer is the work of mission (Sanders, p. 32). To pray is the only way Christians can reach the entire world. Prayer is not the only act of mission that a Christian can do, but it is the greatest thing they can do (Pollard, p. 14).

Prayer meetings

The PCV has a tradition in some local churches whereby a prayer meeting is held every morning. In other areas it is held on Wednesday nights. I think this is a good tradition and it should always be maintained. However, these prayer meetings have become tradition or a duty that needs to be done. Some of these meetings take only 10–15 minutes on prayer, while another 30–45 minutes is spent on singing, preaching and sharing of prayer points. The PCV needs to see prayer time as just a time for prayer. Most people find it hard to spend even an hour in prayer. There are many methods of prayer that can help in prayer time: prayer in small groups, united prayer, prayer in twos, silent prayer, chain prayer, and someone to pray on our behalf.

In these prayer meetings you hardly hear prayer for missionaries and the mission work. The PCV is concerned about its own needs and neglects the needs of the world. It seems that the PCV has lost sight of the purpose of prayer. Too often we see prayer as a systematic time for reading off our list of desires, when in fact prayer is the way we seek not to change God's mind, but for God to change our minds (Pollard, p. 14). I believe that if the PCV wants to be effectively involved in world mission, it has to start with prayer. Prayer is the essential step. It may take months or years of sacrificial, believing prayer before God begins to bring the PCV to the place that it ought to be spiritually.

Prayer intercessors

The PCV should encourage different groups to be involved in intercessory prayer. To start an intercessory prayer group, one needs to be an intercessor oneself. There are different groups in the PCV that should be involved in intercessory prayer for mission: men's fellowship, Presbyterian Women's Missionary Union (PWMU – Women's fellowship), youth group, and Sunday school. Others that would be good to get involved as intercessors are the old and retired people; they have little to do so they should spend their time in praying for missions.

Giving

As the PCV begins to establish goals in missions and to establish plans and programs to carry out such goals, the question soon arises, how will we fund this? This is an area where a lot of Christians would say it is not possible to give to missions because there are lots of ministries in our own churches that also need to be supported financially. When I talk about the PCV, I am not talking about a local church but the denomination. The PCV is the largest denomination in Vanuatu.

How can the PCV say that she cannot support missions with funds? I believe she can. Yes, local rural churches would find it difficult because they depend on relatives in towns to help them with funds. However, that must not be an excuse for the urban churches. There are some good churches in urban areas that could support a missionary themselves. I believe there would be greater support of funds if there were awareness of missions that was built up by three things: pulpit preaching, Christian education, and living with a stewardship mentality.

Mission is the scriptural mandate to the church, so mission finance is part of the mandate. Donald McGavran writes, 'The church ought not to delude itself that great movement in Christ will occur without great commitment of prayer and treasure' (McGavran, pp. 209–12). There is no cheap way to carry out the great commission. The expansion of the church and the spreading of the gospel will not take care of itself. It takes considerable quantities of hard cash and many dedicated Christians who pour themselves into bringing their people into faith and obedience. The PCV would be giving well to missions only if individuals fully give themselves to the Lord. Christian giving begins of course with the giving of our whole life to God in response to all that God has done for us (Romans 12:1).

Going

I would like to challenge the PCV about how John G. Paton came to Vanuatu. Paton was a dropout from Grade 6, but God still used him. Most young people who drop out from Grade 6 often think that they are good for nothing. God can still use them for his ministry if they are willing to say 'Lord, send me'.

Paton was involved in the work of evangelism in his home church. This prepared him for the wider work of evangelism. This is a challenge to pastors who are selecting candidates for the mission course at Talua. They should choose a person who is a 'born-again Christian' and is already involved in a ministry in the church. It is not a good idea to choose a person who has just finished Grade 10 and has had no experience in Church ministry.

Paton faced a lot of opposition from his friends and church members about coming to Vanuatu. The church did not want Paton to leave the wonderful job he was doing in winning souls for Jesus Christ. I believe as the PCV begins to send missionaries overseas, there will be some prominent church leaders who feel that God is calling them to go out as missionaries. The church should not stop them because of their ministry in the church and the loss that would be felt in Vanuatu. The PCV should understand that mission work is for every Christian. Only a few will go but the rest are to pray, to give and to do the ministries at home.

Cross-cultural ministry at home

Since the PCV has sent out so few missionaries to other countries, God is bringing the countries to Vanuatu. There are people from different nationalities in our two towns. There are Asians, Indians, Australians, New Zealanders, Americans, Russians and French. There are some Muslims too, and God has brought to our local communities Peace Corps from different nationalities. There is a great opportunity for cross-cultural ministries at home. The PCV should consider how to minister to these groups of people. Once they become Christian they can be missionaries to their own people.

Short-term mission

In the PCV there have been groups going to different countries, especially to Australia and New Caledonia. But these groups do not see themselves as missionaries. Their main idea is to visit the country and maybe to sing in choirs on Sunday. In the future the PCV should see these groups as short-term missionaries. Short-term mission is a practical way for participants to experience life on the mission field and to test the water concerning a future long-term involvement in mission. The PCV should use short-term missions as an education vehicle for the church. Those who go out need to be trained concerning 'culture shock' and how to maintain quality interpersonal relationships. They need to be briefed about the country and the people they are going to. When they come back from mission work they should debriefed in the local churches.

Tent makers

I am thinking here especially of Vanuatu students who go out to other countries for further studies. The church should encourage them to be aware that they too can play an important role in mission while they are in other countries.

Missionary past

John Paton and other missionaries have already played their part to fulfil the great commission of our Lord to 'go to all the peoples and preach the gospel of Jesus Christ' (Matthew 28:18–20). However, the gospel has not reached all people. This means that the PCV must not only consider building and maintaining her own church, but must seek to reach out to other nations with the gospel. I believe the PCV could send more missionaries out; the unfinished task of reaching the other nations is now in our hands.

The PCV needs revival

The book *Operation World* states that in the PCV there are 13,000 members (Johnstone, p. 575). The membership has grown since 1993.

These members would claim to be Christians, but I wonder how many of them are born-again or committed Christians. Nominalism is one of the problems facing the PCV today. Traditional beliefs and syncretism are evidence of nominalism in the church. However, I must say that there are pockets of revival in the PCV. This revival needs to be developed in order to bring revival to the PCV as a whole. The PCV needs a Christianity that is based on a theology not of quantity and membership but on conversion, personal commitment and spiritual growth. I believe the preparation for the PCV to be involved in mission in the world is to have a spiritual awakening in the church. 'There can be no missionary vision without evangelical zeal; there can be no evangelical zeal without personal purity; there can be no personal purity without genuine conversion experiences' (Kane, p. 77). This I believe is required in the PCV.

Mission-minded pastors

The pastor is an important part of the mission outreach of a church. Yet many pastors in the PCV are not concerned about missions. PCV pastors should be mission minded. Pastors should build congregations or churches that exist as a centre for equipping Christians for the work of evangelism and mission. World mission cannot take place without a community of believers who are on fire for world mission. The local church cannot be on fire if the pastor is not missionary minded. World mission starts from a pastor and his local church. The local church is the agent of fulfilling the purpose of God to evangelise the world.

Conclusion

For the PCV to be effectively involved in mission, I believe it should become World Christian. This would involve, first of all, revival in the church. I believe nothing can change the perspective of the church for mission or bring to life the vision of mission in the lives and hearts of the PCV except a new moving of the Holy Spirit. The PCV should continue to emphasise personal conversion, growing in discipleship and prayer life that would lead to a church that is committed and dedicated to the work of God's mission. Secondly, it would involve biblical teaching about mission. The PCV needs to understand God's purpose for the world. This could be done through preaching, teaching, Bible studies and mobilising about missions, through praying, giving, and encouraging others to go. I believe God is going to use the PCV to be effectively involved in mission only if the PCV is willing to take up these challenges.

Bibliography

Johnstone, P. J., editor, *Operation World: A Handbook for World Intercession*, 5th edition, Kent: Operation Mobilization, 1998

Kane, J. B., *A Concise History of the Christian World Mission*, Grand Rapids, Michigan: Baker, 1978

McGavran, Donald, *Momentous Decisions in Missions Today*, Grand Rapids, Michigan: Baker, 1993

Pollard, Mike, editor, *Cultivating a Mission-active Church*, Wheaton: ACMC, 1990

Sanders, Oswald, *Effective Evangelism: The Divine Art of Soul-winning*, Georgia: Operation Mobilization, 1982

A Concept of Mission in Vanuatu

Noclam Olivier

Introduction

Today the majority of ni-Vanuatu recognise themselves as Christians. However, the reality within each individual is slightly different from what most of the people may see and understand. There are two types of Christians. The first are the older generations who may not know and would not accept the idea of inculturation; they see Christianity as having a Western fabric and have no strong sense or feeling of belonging to a Vanuatu church. The second are the younger generations who are open to changes in the church; they easily find their place in the structural Vanuatu church.

The life of the Christian churches in Vanuatu and the spread and the acceptance of the gospel in the future will depend very much on the attitudes of the missionaries and church activists towards the culture. In this essay I, as a ni-Vanuatu, will emphasise and uncover two ways for today's mission in Vanuatu traditional society to proceed, namely Apology and Inculturation. These two methods cannot be separated from each other because one enhances the other. However to clarify some of the points, I will also speak of my own cross-culture experience.

1. Apology

Past Experience

The attitude of the early missionaries has left the old ni-Vanuatu still wondering about the essence of Christianity today. Most of the first missionaries who arrived in Vanuatu last century totally denied and opposed the existence of the indigenous culture. There was no dialogue between traditional religions and biblical revelation. They were merely nationalists trying to enforce and establish their own identity. They were concerned about the imperial interests of the home government. The gospel of Christ was preached in Western perspectives, what some anthropologists describe as 'Western missionaries monologue'. English and French missionaries were disrespectful of the local cultures, imposing their religious customs. The native peoples were forced to abandon their cultures: languages, symbols, rituals, dances and practices that were normal to them, in order to join Western Christianity.

A lot of indigenous people were bitter and they were punished for trying to defend their own identity. On the Island of Tanna, a number of people were tied up to a tree and left standing for a day and night by Christian followers (Bonnemaison Joel, *Tanna les Hommes Lieux*, Paris: Edition de L'orstom, 1987, p. 436). Despite the brutality of the followers of the Christian religion, ni-Vanuatu people managed to keep alive their culture and their identity. It has been part of their being; the culture is rooted in their hearts.

Today a lot of people refer to that period and those missionaries by describing them as 'being missionaries of their own times'. However, what they forget to look at is the culture itself and the people affected during this period. This is one of the essential issues in Vanuatu Christian society. A lot of indigenous people who experienced this happening are the main bearers of the culture today. They are people who once were victims, but are now the pillars of the traditional society.

For the church to introduce a true and reliable inculturation, she has to adapt herself first of all to the bearers of the culture, that is, to those who are the traditional leaders or chiefs. They have the great advantage of being culturally conditioned for the environment in which they operate, they understand its people, speak the local tongue and share the local way of life.

Today's challenge

One of the biggest challenges existing today in the traditional society is well known to the first group of people I mentioned earlier in the introduction: the older generation. They are the cornerstone of our tradition. I remember one evening, during the preparation of my brother's wedding, I told the chief of our village that I would bring some cultural elements into the liturgy such as dances and costumes, to make the celebration more meaningful and local. But he could not accept it. He rejected it by saying, 'The wedding in the chapel is a church wedding; everything has to be done in Western style, and you should not mix religion and culture'.

From this moment I realised that there is something still alive in the heart of the old people. I came to understand that there is one thing that the church has forgotten to look at, especially in relation to the old people who had experienced the brutality of the early Christian followers, and that is reconciliation. Our chief had often been attending worship celebration on Sunday, but never wanted to be baptised. This is real, and this is only one of many cases that exist in traditional Vanuatu society.

New mission

Culture is becoming very important for today's evangelism. Ni-Vanuatu are very passionate about their own cultures. Whatever their denomination or organization, whoever takes account of their culture becomes part of the culture. Nevertheless, the church today has not been humble enough to explain her past and apologise to the older generations. In most of ni-Vanuatu society, the Christian churches have been regarded as master and not as servant. This mentality has kept the old people silent or passive about their hurts, their pasts and their true feeling toward the Christian churches. As a consequence of this, the outcome is often an unreadiness to accept the Christian faith, or a spiritual immaturity as Christians. They are not ready to unveil and join in the inculturation of the church. They have not really encountered the fullness of Christian revelation.

Today in most of the villages there will not be a reliable, applicable and true inculturation unless the role of the church in the minds of the people changes from master to a humble servant. In many places such as Tanna, there is a need for an apology. There is a need for individual and group healing, and restoration of the humanity that earlier missionaries tried to destroy. The Christian churches in some parts of Vanuatu have to be renewed and founded on a more solid understanding of respect and dialogue with indigenous culture.

2. Inculturation

I understand inculturation as the integration of the gospel with a particular culture. It is an outgoing process or dialogue between gospel and culture. In other words, it is a call to continuous conversion and renewal and a grounding of Christian faith in concrete and particular circumstances.

To practice inculturation in Vanuatu is not as straightforward as people may think. The culture itself is very complicated; the question of what elements may be accepted and what have to be rejected is always hard to answer. Many people still strongly believe that what is cultural is evil for Christians, and therefore they hardly reveal the roots behind the leaves. What is real and true about certain cultural activities is unknown, for instance, why men have participated in the drinking of kava and women were not allowed.

However, to come to a certain conclusion one has to follow a certain pattern. The paschal mystery of Christ, his life, death and resurrection is vital in understanding the process of inculturation. The processes of listening, surrendering and not being judgemental are very essential in understanding ni-Vanuatu culture.

Stranger-death

As a missionary, I have to go beyond myself in order to understand and empathise with the indigenous people in completely different situations. I surrender my whole self and let my being be driven by the new situation. Its social, political and economical systems are very important. I have to be a humble person ready to listen, explore, learn and be able to change when the reality tells me. I must become a stranger and do so with dignity. I have no power to impose my own authority or try to take control of the cultural system. In the past, missionaries have often reacted strongly to reverse their status as 'stranger' as quickly as possible, demanding to be treated with respect, as guests or God-bringer. Whatever confusion I myself feel, I must acknowledge my responsibility to allow the ni-Vanuatu the freedom and the grace to be themselves.

However, to feel a stranger in certain circumstances is very unpleasant. It is a very painful situation to be in, but very rewarding at the end of the process. For instance, my first experience of a cross-culture situation was when I moved to Sydney in 1996. I had culture shock and was very confused in the beginning. In the first two months, I surrendered myself to Western cultural patterns, I accepted hospitality and tried to be gracious while learning to be sensitive to the nuances and the feelings of others in my situation of transition. I became an alien among the myths of another people, not knowing what to do, what to eat, how to communicate, and how to move and interact in my new milieu.

It was a period of openness, listening and receiving. My whole attitude allowed other people to interact with me. I was able to indicate my openness, my integrity and willingness to engage in relationship. Nevertheless, during this period, I ignored my culture, my language and my whole self in experiencing the new culture. I was hoping that in the future I would enjoy the Western culture in the same way as I do to my own culture. I died in order to find myself in a new creation, a new beginning.

New beginning – Resurrection

New beginning is the period when I master the language and become familiar with the culture, its tradition and the roots behind the leaves. There is a similar process involved in analysing Christianity and culture and combining them in order to create a clear and meaningful Christian faith. The decision about what in the culture is acceptable and has to be taken up, or what is not acceptable and has to be left out, needs to take place. As we know in Vanuatu, not every cultural element is considered good; some can kill and destroy, others can give life or healing.

The Christian faith can now be grounded in concrete and particular circumstances in our culture; the struggle is over. As a missionary I should now be able to form a new church identity as a truly local Christian, in a church that exists within her own time and place, in a church that reflects the relationship between the gospel and traditional values.

In my own cross-cultural experience this is the period when I started to enjoy vegemite and share my own gifts and talents as a ni-Vanuatu with other people in my own community in Australia. Resurrection or Incarnation is the final process of inculturation. Culture and Christianity now speak the same language and use the same symbols, ritual and spirituality. The Word of God is incarnate in the new culture and the indigenous people can relate to it and understand it in their own ways. This process allows the church to become local by developing its own structures, art forms, liturgies, ministry and theology.

Conclusion

The task of mission in Vanuatu is very important. Apology and Inculturation are the main ideas for mission today in traditional societies. They cannot be separated from each other. If a missionary ignores the apology to indigenous people, he will also ignore the church and its relationship to their true culture, their myths and their customs. The apology strengthens the relationship between church and culture and allows a solid and reliable inculturation to immerge. The paschal mystery of Christ is very central and has to be considered as a model for today's inculturation. The role of a humble servant is very fundamental for the Christian churches to consider. Ni-Vanuatu often regard the Christian church as a master. This mentality has often limited their openness to take part freely in the church today.

Justice, Peace and Love in Contemporary Melanesia

Stanley Ure

Introduction

I would like to present my point of view on the status of justice, peace and love in contemporary society, basing these on my cultural background, Christian principles, constitutional obligation and my observations and experiences as a lay person, a community developer, a theological student, a church minister and now a teacher at a theological institution. My presentation is based mainly on Vanuatu, with which I am most familiar. However, I believe that there are a lot of similarities between Vanuatu and the rest of Melanesia.

I would also like to examine critically the relationship between indigenous and modern values and concepts, and how these relate to creating the environment for sustainable justice, peace and love at village level, national level, and across Melanesia, and how these relate to religion and government. Let me begin by identifying the existing principles that direct the values and conduct of justice, peace and love.

Principles of justice, peace and love

Truth, justice, peace, human rights and freedom are collectively owned. Individual rights involve having the right to parental care, to be loved, to be taught, to be fed, to be housed, to be disciplined, to have access to land, to live in peace, and to belong to the extended family for social security.

Peace is paramount and is collectively owned. It is built on indigenous value systems and relationships. It becomes the central focus to all conduct of activities. Truth and justice are conditions for peace. Individual rights, freedom and obligations are exercised and practiced within the parameters of discipline and collectivity. The whole society takes responsibility for nurturing, educating and teaching. This responsibility begins in the family home with a commitment to ensure that families respect peace, especially in the way they talk, act and behave with each other.

The Christian principles of justice, peace and love are provided for in the Ten Commandments. The Ten Commandments guide human justice and morality and are consistent with the creation laws.

The Vanuatu national constitution supervises the conduct of modern governance and monitors the state of fundamental rights to freedom, justice and peace. Today all constitutions, laws and regulations in Melanesia are based on British Common Law, and French Law in New Caledonia. Our biggest challenge is to understand the interpretation of the constitution and the laws and how these relate to natural justice, natural peace and natural love.

Value systems that sustain contemporary societies

The indigenous philosophy of life is to co-exist peacefully with everyone and with everything that shares the multi-dimensional natural world of interdependence. Spirituality is alive among the people and is a resource for guidance in all they do. All their activities are conducted with respect towards the upholding of peace in their community.

Indigenous peoples have always recognised the integrity and dignity of individual persons or a group of human persons as fundamental human rights. This is centrally linked to fundamental collective rights to self-determination, independence and sovereignty.

Governance in the indigenous context is the management of communities to maintain a commitment to social security, economic self-reliance and political stability. The natural principles of good governance have always played a major role in sustaining our communities at all levels of Melanesian society. It begins in family homes, where the nurturing of truth, justice, peace, love, community life and responsibilities has its origin. Democracy, leadership and authority become a collective activity to ensure that justice is upheld and peace is respected, protected and monitored to serve the well-being of all in the society.

Leadership is nurtured and groomed at an early age and continues throughout adulthood. Leaders are spiritually guided with skills, knowledge and the acquiring of wisdom needed for their role in coordinating and monitoring the state of peace at all levels and in all institutions, including the family, clan, tribe, village, island and national communities. Quality leadership, authority and good governance are measured by the ability to provide for individual and collective needs, and to uphold a cohesive community spirit, the state of peace and human security, and the feeling of social security, economic self-reliance and political stability.

All activities are conducted openly and all information is for public consumption, to keep the communities well informed. Anything that may contribute to disturbing individual, family or community cohesiveness is properly scrutinised and corrected prior to it being presented to the community. Community gatherings and meetings are for the free participation of all members of the community. They become a learning place for the whole community, where individual intelligence and wisdom are exchanged. Decisions are taken collectively. Indigenous knowledge, skills, talents and wisdom are used for community needs and are transmitted orally to the next generation.

Any disturbance to peace is frowned upon and collective responsibility to restore the peace becomes urgent. The leader takes responsibility to compensate for peace on behalf of his community. Truth, justice, peace and love are based on the indigenous philosophy of life that respects peaceful co-existence as paramount in life. This is the way of life that is being taught in indigenous education and implemented in indigenous communities.

The Melanesian concept of education is linked to the development philosophy and vision of Melanesia, as it is in any cultural context. Education is a lifetime process that begins at conception and only stops when one dies. The origin of any education system is linked to a creation story, the foundation of a belief system and spirituality that directs the mode of production and the evolving environment in which we live or have lived over the centuries up to now.

An individual is educated in their natural environment by people who surround them, including their parents, older peers, clan members, community chiefs, skilful and talented members of the society, and wise men and women of the older generation. Education is about everything that people come into contact in everyday life and it teaches practical skills for their roles in society and for their responsibilities at different stages of human development. It is all connected to natural laws that nurture natural peace, human values, truth, respect, justice, quality leadership and economic production. Each person learns what is needed in life to be socially secure and economically self-supporting.

Education is more than what is provided in a classroom situation. In a natural situation it is commonly said that a mother is the first teacher, while parents provide the education foundation within the family before a child moves on and receives further knowledge and skills within a wider community. This concept encompasses the cultural and traditional environment under which the people have lived in harmony and survived over centuries as communities.

Peace is nurtured and taught within the family and the community to ensure that the words that are spoken, the actions taken and the attitudes portrayed are conducted with respect to natural laws and protocols, and do not disturb the spirit of peace within an individual, family, tribe or community. Every individual is taught their individual rights and freedoms and how, where, when and to what extent these can be practiced within the context of collective rights and freedom. It becomes a natural obligation to take collective responsibility as a community member, sharing and caring for the welfare and sustainable livelihood of all. It also teaches and encourages people to take control of their own lives so that they can determine their own social, economic and political status.

Prior to the arrival of Christian missionaries, justice, peace and love were guided by the creation laws of society. During the process of evolution, the first species that inhabited the universe and the planet made the first natural laws based on the creation law. Natural laws are there to uphold peace. According to my own cultural creation story, human beings were the latest species that inhabited this planet and they therefore made what is today known as customary law. From my own indigenous history there are six laws of the land that make up the customary law. These regulate, supervise and monitor peaceful co-existence. Unfortunately none of these laws were taken into account when Pacific countries drafted their constitutions and laws.

Issues of justice, peace and love

Melanesian issues in the twenty-first century are still connected to the events that began in the fifteenth century and continued on through history without being properly resolved with mutual respect. The scope of the issues has increased both proportionally and in complexity. We are reminded of our responsibilities in redefining what life holds for our future generation.

The soul of Melanesia continues to search for its natural identity and natural values that uphold natural peace. This is done among value conflicts, religious conflicts, relationship conflicts, information conflicts, institutional and structural conflicts, leadership and democratic conflicts, economic-interest conflicts and, most importantly, in land and cultural conflicts. These conflicts and crises are not coincidental, and must be seen as the soul of Melanesia in constant pain. Sometimes it is crying out aloud and warning us to redefine our peaceful co-existence with others who share the land and environment with us, to re-examine our past, to pay respect where it is due in order to heal the past damage and to restore the natural elements needed for the future generations to inherit a just and peaceful society.

Unfortunately, the collective rights of Melanesian people that have sustained peaceful communities for centuries are not adequately legalised in national constitutions, modern laws and international treaties to safeguard values of collective ownership. National constitutions and international human rights concepts seem to put more emphasis on individual rights and freedom without limits. Legally recognised individual freedom and rights that go beyond collective rights have always been a cause of community conflict.

Over the centuries our societies have encountered different waves of ideological invasion. One of these is the introduction of the Christian religion and the Bible. While Christianity and modernisation have had an impact on our Melanesian societies, people still value indigenous beliefs and their spiritual links to the land, which supervise their social conduct and political relationships. Modern constitutions and laws that attempt to respond to fundamental human rights issues that are spiritually linked to the roots and the soul of Melanesian communities have always met with challenges. In trying to govern Melanesian communities there is always conflict with customary laws and value systems. Melanesian people more often become victims than beneficiaries of foreign introduced laws.

When independence was achieved among Melanesian countries, we only replaced white faces with black faces, but we inherited the same Western systems, institutions, governance, leadership, authority and model of capitalist development associated with a Western philosophy of life. I often question myself as to the appropriateness of these forms to Melanesian societies. The major problem has been the absence of visionary leaders with political will to interpret international Christian principles, modern constitutions and laws to bring about natural justice, natural peace and natural love in societies.

Modern education and modern life do not offer justice, peace and love. They have created chaos, insecurity and poverty over against the Melanesian spirit of caring and sharing. Therefore when Melanesia rebels against the system, a new model of life based on indigenous values and modern values should be offered.

Disturbance to peace is reported to the police or the army and the Western system of justice is used to hear the cases. Some cases take months or years to deal with, resulting in more disturbances to peace. Melanesia is ruled by this system because it has been defined as part of what is termed a 'civilised and democratic free society'.

Western military strategies for peace in Melanesia are vested in weapons, in the use of security forces, and in those who control the decision-making process. Governments feel more secure with the police and the army, while political affiliations become targets in armed conflicts. Internal militarisation of independent island nations has increased with an increase in military budgets and police spending. Decision-makers and planners do not plan for genuine peace, but continue to put emphasis on Western military models of security, which are expensive and are offered as part of bilateral/multilateral packages. Recent examples are shown by the conflict in Bougainville, the Solomon Islands, the coups and mutiny in the Fiji Islands, armed clashes and attempted mutiny in Papua New Guinea and Vanuatu, and the build up of tensions in other countries.

Additional growing threats are faced by Melanesian peoples and their environment through climate change and rising sea levels, destructive mining and logging.

The way forward

In assessing the existing guiding principles, I would say that Melanesia is rich in the knowledge needed to nurture a just society where peace and love prevail. The question then is how to transfer the existing knowledge through Christian teaching and formal education to mould the kind of citizens and leaders who will continue to promote truth, justice, peace and love.

Today Melanesian societies need visionary and quality national leaders who uphold spiritual values for life: family values, cohesive community spirit, genuine states of peace, social security, economic self-reliance, and political stability. Such leaders need, in their exercise of authority and good governance, to command the respect of people under their jurisdiction. Indigenous systems of respect, collective ownership, responsibility, transparency and accountability to peaceful co-existence mark the way forward towards natural justice, peace and love. This proved to have worked in the initiation of peace processes in Bougainville, Solomon Islands, Fiji and Vanuatu. However, these need to be integrated into mainstream education.

We should attempt to interpret and translate national constitutions and modern laws in all schools. We need to use Melanesian values in determining our future security. We need to use our indigenous concepts of collective ownership of ecological biodiversity, rights, freedom, community responsibility, public information, open communication, truth and justice as the foundation for our peaceful co-existence in Melanesia.

We must also reform the national education system and curricula to enhance our Melanesian values of collective ownership of human rights, truth, peace, love and human security, which are the pillars for peaceful co-existence. Together with young women and men, mothers and fathers, traditional leaders, church leaders and government leaders, we must take full responsibility to appropriately nurture and guide the human population within the families, in the communities and at national level to uphold truth, natural justice, peace and love. Only then can we hope for a transformed Melanesian society based on both the Melanesian values of justice and human rights, and the introduced values that are friendly to peaceful co-existence.

This paper was first delivered to the second Contextual Conference of Melanesian Theologians in Honiara, Solomon Islands, in 2004.

Understanding the Gospel in Vanuatu: The Impact of Globalisation

John Leung

Despite its remoteness in the South Pacific and with only 200,000 ni-Vanuatu people scattered over 83 islands, the budding young Melanesian nation of Vanuatu is not insulated in any way from globalisation.[4] The impact of globalisation from the mid-1980s onwards has brought about an increasing socio-economic impoverishment of the majority of small nations around the Pacific Rim, and Vanuatu is not exempted.[5] As a result of the increased interconnectedness in the various fields of technology and communication, the ni-Vanuatu of this generation have found themselves the prime target of exploitation by a few greedy and corrupted people from within and abroad.[6]

Certain Western cults have taken advantage of this globalisation and tried to proselytise, especially in the southern islands of Vanuatu. One would have expected that with globalisation the invasion of these Western cults would carry the spiritual battle to a new height.[7] A survey of the past 150 years of Christianity in Vanuatu has indicated that there is a constant paradigmatic shift in the understanding of the proclamation of the gospel over the decades and on the way it is received. It is the purpose of this essay to discern what shift there may be in the understanding of the proclamation of the gospel and to see how this perception has affected the way the gospel is being received now.[8]

Factors countering the negative impact of globalisation in the understanding of the gospel

With the arrival of foreign religions (such as Islam in the southern island of Efate) and the Western cults through globalisation, one would have expected an increased confusion and pollution in the understanding of the proclamation of the gospel. This possibility has been counteracted successfully to a large extent by the following factors. First and foremost is the Vanuatu Council of Churches, which is able to maintain the firm foundation laid down by missionaries of the past 150 years.[9] The sound footing in biblical knowledge has been invaluable in preventing the advances of the various cultic movements from forming a firm stranglehold upon the church leaders.[10] In a study of the answers to the sixteen questions asked of leaders in a survey on their understanding of the Christian faith, it appeared that they showed a fairly reasonable and evangelical understanding of the Christian God and the gospel.[11] Ongoing religious education, such as that conducted by Talua Ministry Training Centre in Santo, Vanuatu, is a vital strategic means of training future pastors not only for the Presbyterian Church of Vanuatu, but also for the Church of Melanesia, the Church of Christ in Vanuatu, and other evangelical churches of the South Pacific Basin nations.[12] This sound theological heritage and training is one of the key factors in preventing Western cults from taking root in Vanuatu in the twenty-first century.[13]

Another important consideration is the strength of the evangelical church polity in Vanuatu and their alliance not only with one another but also with other non-evangelical churches that also confess the Apostolic or similar Creed.[14] Through the contractual agreement between Anglican Bishop Selwyn and the Presbyterian John Geddie in the 1840s and beyond, the region was strategically divided up into two large mission fields, with the Anglicans primarily responsible for evangelism in the northern islands and the Presbyterians in the south.[15] Presbyterian Church polity has established a closely-knit network of governance, so that information regarding any cultic activity can be readily shared and action taken through collective wisdom. The fact that there had been precedence with the invasion of a religious cult in the mid-1940s was a distinct advantage in immunising Vanuatu against any spiritual invasion through globalisation in the twenty-first century. John Frum's Cargo Cult of the 1940s in the southern island of Tanna has allowed the evangelical churches to be constantly on the alert and be ready and quick to respond to the introduction of any cults since that time.[16] Although this cult is still active in Vanuatu, its members are dwindling and are confined mainly to the island of Tanna in the south of the country. Of course, one must not overlook the important work done by evangelical missionaries and the Bible translators over the past two decades. They have been working laboriously in remote villages in the various islands of Vanuatu, teaching the illiterate indigenous ni-Vanuatu a written form of their oral customs and diverse languages.[17]

Having a firm foundation of biblical truth and a strong polity at the local level are good guards against any subsequent epidemic of cultic outbreaks.

How the gospel is understood in the light of globalisation

Even before the coming of the pioneer missionaries in the mid-nineteenth century, the ni-Vanuatu have always held the notion of a supreme, good and generous deity (also known traditionally as Tagaro on Pentecost island).[18] They believe the cosmic evil spirits live in graveyards and sacred places, and interfere with human affairs when humans intrude upon their territory. Appeasement and sacrifices to the spirits and gods are then required for reconciliation. Over the past 150 years, and through the work of the missionaries, they have come to a full knowledge and understanding of the one and true Creator God through faith in Jesus Christ alone.[19] In a 1995 survey by the Council of Churches in Vanuatu, it appeared they have a sound confession of the understanding of the triune Christian God.[20] They knew the only way to the one true God is by trusting in Jesus Christ as Saviour and to worship the Father only through him and in the Holy Spirit. This is the belief of the majority of ni-Vanuatu Christians.

However, as a result of globalisation, especially in remote island villages, there are signs of Christians being attracted to a 'prosperity' gospel. The Mormons, Bahai and Jehovah Witnesses are becoming a threat to the traditional Christian churches. They are active in 'luring people into their temples with promises of money, clothing and other material goods'.[21] In areas where the Word of God is weak and poverty is extreme, 'Christianity and modern Western businesses' become good bedfellows, but frequently at the expense of a pollution of the gospel message.

Another notable feature in the understanding of the gospel in this age of globalisation in Vanuatu is that there is a certain degree of Christian nominalism amongst the Christians through 'communal conversion'. It still holds true in the twenty-first century that 'once a tribal chief agreed to accept the gospel then it meant the entire community will turn to Christianity.'[22] This is inherent in their tribal tradition, where the village chief (and at times the head of a family clan) has absolute and totalitarian authority over all the constituents subordinate to him. This lack of a personal commitment to Christ, is a reason for the nominalism amongst Christians of this age. For this group of people, being a Christian means going to church on Sundays and joining community and other church activities, but without a full grasp of the grace of God in Jesus or of a personal commitment to Christ as Saviour and Lord. Statistics on this group of Christians are hard to come by.

Johnny Naual, in his article on conversion, also noted a third group of Christians in Vanuatu – those with a syncretistic view of the

Christian faith. Naual regards syncretism not so much as a worshiping of a number of gods in addition to the Christian God, but as the combination of belief in Jesus Christ with traditional superstition. It is true one can overcome this through continual pastoral care and teaching of the Scripture to these predominantly illiterate communities. In areas where witchcraft and voodoo still have a hold on the village people, their faith in Christ as victor and conqueror over demons is of particular comfort to them. But once again old superstitious religious beliefs take time and courage and reassurance to overcome.

In the area of application of their understanding of the gospel in the current age, much globalisation has taken place. With the rise of nationalism since independence in 1980, church leaders in Vanuatu are keen to blend their traditional customs and practices with Christianity. Much has been written to promote the Christian faith in the areas of dress, marriage, death and burial, and issues with kava, feasting, sacrifices and ceremonial offerings. Some of these customs may have an religious undertone and evangelical church leaders have been at pains to try to resolve these issues.[23]

A privately prepared concoction of holy water is still being used by certain pastors in hospitals and pastoral visits for anointing the sick in Vanuatu. There is a certain degree of tolerance of such practices in the church for the healing of the sick and infirmed. Frequently it is difficult to obtain bread and wine or grape juice for the Lord's Supper, hence coconut milk and its flesh has been used as a substitute for the elements in the Lord's Supper. However, they do not consider the elements as transubstantiation, but as a means to remember the love of God in Christ as a once for all and final sacrifice. They partake in the Lord's Supper as the body and blood of Christ and to do it in remembrance of his death on the cross.[24] This would be a good example of an inculturation of the gospel with traditional customs and belief. It is therefore seen that not only was cannibalism abandoned for the sake of the gospel, widow-strangling, infanticide and polygamy have also given way in the light of the understanding and application of the gospel. Although polygamy is still practiced by a few men in power as a status symbol, it is no longer seen as a valid tradition by Christians. In their enthusiasm in enculturating their traditions with the gospel however, there are times when the issue seems somewhat artificial and forced.[25]

Their awareness of the pollution caused by the invasion of the religious cults in the era of globalisation is a sign of their maturity in Vanuatu. The measures taken by the people to counterbalance the cultic pollution is an indication of their understanding of the importance of the Christian faith in their lives. It indicates not only an understanding, but also its relevance. The fact that the laws and customs were amended according to biblical teaching testifies to their earnest commitment to the Christian faith.[26]

How the gospel is received

As a result of globalisation there is a dramatic shift in the perception and subsequent reception of the proclamation of the gospel. Because of the increased inter-connectedness amongst nations, the ni-Vanuatu have developed an increased awareness of the need to equip themselves even better in an evangelical understanding of the Word. This was necessary in the light of an ever increasing and confusing spiritual milieu brought about by the various religious cults from globalised nations. Not only has there been an increase in the invasion of cultic activities into Vanuatu, there has also been a corresponding increase in the demand, commitment and response by and from various global evangelical mission societies, evangelical missionary organisations and Bible translators since the 1990s.[27] This coincided roughly with the period of the rise of nationalism since independence in July 1980. Local church leaders not only openly embraced an evangelical stand on the gospel, but they also strived for a higher degree of contextualisation, adaptation, accommodation and globalisation of the gospel with their old traditions, customs and even religious beliefs.[28]

A review of the historical development of the early missionaries to the New Hebrides is essential for an understanding of this paradigmatic shift in the reception of the proclamation. When Christianity was first brought to the New Hebrides in 1839, the missionaries were looked upon as 'invaders'. It was therefore little wonder that early missionary pioneers of the London Missionary Society were martyred soon after their arrival.[29] They were considered foreign invaders who came to destroy traditional customs and culture, religious beliefs and ceremonies. Because of their cannibalism and animist worship, these Pacific Islanders were regarded by the missionaries of the 1840s as savages and their customs and culture as heathen and demonic, if not satanic. Missionaries of the 1850s, such as John Geddie, considered that their prime calling in mission was to convert these local inhabitants to live a 'more Christian and civilised' form of life.[30]

Over the course of time and through their witnessing as converters, these missionaries were no longer perceived by the village chiefs as 'invaders' coming to destroy, but rather as 'converters' of their belief system. There was much difficulty at the start, as these missionaries tried to persuade the local chiefs not only to abolish their traditional practices of polygamy, infanticide and widow-strangling, but also to change the pattern of relationships between a man and a woman, and to alter their unquestioned loyalty to their extended family members, regardless of their deeds as immoral or amoral.[31] The traditional practice is of unswerving commitment of family members to one another, and this takes precedence over all moral and other issues. This had led to much infighting between different tribes and family clans in the mid-nineteenth century. Geddie was able to take advantage of this and adopt a conciliatory role as he approached these quarrelling family clans. By contextualising the gospel message of reconciliation in Christ, he was able to bring peace between them. On the issue of local tradition, Geddie's policy was to 'guard against offending the traditional customs of the people. He did this not because the customs had any intrinsic value, but because it was paramount to develop good relations with the people so that they might be more open to hear the missionary message.'[32] As a result, Geddie and others were successful in presenting the missionary image as one of 'converter' rather than as 'invader'.

Such was the local understanding of the gospel in the late-nineteenth and early-twentieth century, and this was an essential and preliminary step in the advancement of the proclamation of the gospel at the time.[33]

The perception of the missionaries' role took a more dramatic turn in the mid- and late-twentieth century as the local church leaders and village chiefs referred to the missionaries as 'transformers' of their traditional culture. The missionaries were no longer referred to as invaders of their traditions or as converters of their ancestral customs and ceremonies, but now as 'transformers'. The people are more receptive to the gospel and more willing to contextualise and to accommodate their traditional culture to the Christian faith. This is particularly so in the area of marriage and family life, where the Christian faith works alongside their traditions and customs. This inculturation of the Christian faith is a positive step by the Vanuatu evangelical churches as they interact proactively with the Christian faith in their daily lives and ceremonies. There is no longer the perception of this being an imposition of Western culture, and the indigenous church leaders have come of age in developing their own specific application of the gospel. However, with this inculturation process was an inherent tendency to revert to their old traditions and customs and syncretisms. Because of the firm biblical foundation set by the early missionary pioneers and coupled with a strong link between the evangelical church leaders and a strong church polity, syncretistic practice has not been a significant issue at this stage.[34] This strong communication between the evangelical churches in Vanuatu has been time-tested by the Cargo Cult of the 1940s. With the rising influence of globalisation in the twenty-first century and the invasion of Western religious cults, this country has an evangelical understanding of the gospel that is being received as having an increasingly transforming role with regard to their old traditions and religious beliefs.

Conclusion

Despite the negative effect of globalisation upon the proclamation of the gospel through the arrival of cults, the ni-Vanuatu people maintain an evangelical understanding and application of the biblical truth. Because of their firm foundation in the Word of God, the gospel is considered and received as a transformer of their traditional customs and practices. This is a radical paradigmatic shift in their reception of the gospel and is a sign of the maturity of these churches.

Bibliography

Armstrong, E. S., *The Melanesian Mission*, London: Isbister, 1900

Beckwith, R. T. & Selman, M. J., *Sacrifices in the Bible*, London: publisher, 1995

Bosch, D. J., *Transforming Mission: Paradigm Shifts in Theology of Mission*, Maryknoll, NY: Orbis, 2002

Dowsett, R., *The Great Commission*, Monarch: Kregel, 2002

Engel, J. & Dyrness, W., *Changing the Mind of Missions: Where Have We Gone Wrong?*, Grand Rapids: IVP, 2000

Friedman, T. L., *The Lexus and the Olive Tree: Understanding Globalisation*, Farrar, Strauss: Giroux, 1999

Garrett, J., *To Live Among the Stars*, Geneva: WCC Publishers, 1982

Gillian, H. R., *Vanuatu Victory: Four Generations of Sharing Christian Faith in the Pacific*, Warburton, Victoria: Spectrum, 1988

Hillard, D., *God's Gentlemen: A History of the Melanesian Mission 1849–1942*, Brisbane: University of Queensland Press, 1978

Hutchinson, M. & Kalu, O., *A Global Faith: Essays on Evangelism and Globalization*, Sydney: Openbook, 1998

Huntington, S. P., *The Clash of Civilizations and the Remaking of World Order*, Place: Touchstone, 1996

Jenkins, P., *The Next Christendom: The Coming of Global Christianity*, London: Oxford University Press, 2002

Miller, J. G., *Live Books 1–6*, Sydney: Presbyterian Church of Australia, 2001

Newbigin, L., *Foolishness to the Greeks: The Gospel and Western Culture*, Grand Rapids: Eerdmans, 1986

Newbigin, L., *The Gospel in a Pluralist Society*, Grand Rapids: Eerdmans, 1989

O'Byrne & Harcombe, *Vanuatu*, 3rd edition, Melbourne: Lonely Planet Publications, 1999

Prior, R., *World Council of Churches Study Process on Gospel and Cultures*, Santo, Vanuatu: Talua Ministry Training Centre, 1995

Prior, R., *Gospel and Culture in Vanuatu: The Founding Missionary and a Missionary for Today*, Melbourne: Gospel Vanuatu Books, 1998

Prior, R., editor, *Gospel and Culture in Vanuatu 2: Contemporary Local Perspectives*, Melbourne: Gospel Vanuatu Books, 2001

Prior, R., editor, *Gospel and Culture in Vanuatu 3: The Voice of the Local Church*, Melbourne: Gospel Vanuatu Books, 2003

Ramachandra, V., *Gods That Fail: Modern Idolatry and Christian Mission*, Grand Rapids: IVP, 1996

Smith, D., *Mission after Christendom*, London: DLT, 2003

Stackhouse, M. L. & Browning, D. S., *God and Globalization: The Spirit and the Modern Authorities*, Volume 2, Harrisburg: Trinity Press International, 2001

Tanihi, E., *Relating the Gospel to Traditional Melanesia Belief*, a research paper and exit thesis from Talua Ministry Centre, Santo, Vanuatu, May 2004

Taylor, J. V., *The Scattered Self*, London: The Prime Vision, 1963

Taylor, W. D., *Too Valuable to Lose: Exploring the Causes and Cures of Missionary Attrition*, Pasadena, California: William Carey, 1997

Taylor, W. D., editor, *Global Missiology for the 21st Century: The Iguassu Dialogue*, Grand Rapids: Baker, 2000

Tiplady, R., editor, *One World or Many: The Impact of Globalisation on Missions*, Pasadena: William Carey Library, 2003

Tiplady, R., editor, *Postmission: Mission by a Post-Modern Generation*, Place: Paternoster, 2003

Tippett, A. R., *The Deep Sea Canoe Stories of the Spread of the Gospel by South Pacific Island Missionaries*, Wewak, PNG: Wirui Press, 1994

Trompf, G., editor, *The Gospel is Not Western*, Maryknoll, NY: Orbis, 1987

Walls, A. E., *The Missionary Movement in Christian History: Studies in the Transmission of Faith*, Melbourne: Orbis, 1997

Webber, R. E., *Ancient-Future Faith: Rethinking Evangelicalism for a Postmodern World*, Grand Rapids: Baker Books, 1999

Webber, R. E., *The Younger Evangelicals: Facing the Challenges of the New World*, Grand Rapids: Baker, 2002

Whiteman, D., *An Introduction to Melanesian Cultures*, Goroka, PNG: Melanesian Institute, 1984

Wright, C. & Fugui, L., editors, *Christ in South Pacific Cultures*, Suva, Fuji: Lotu Pasifica, 1985

Van Der Veer, P., *Conversion to Modernities: The Globalisation of Modernity*, London: Routledge, 1996

Verstraelen, F. J., editor, *Missiology: An Ecumenical Introduction Texts and contents of Global Christianity*, Grand Rapids: Eerdmans, 1995

Strategies for Proclamation of the Gospel in a Globalised Vanuatu

John Leung

Introduction

In 1993, Samuel Huntington predicted the strong possibility of a clash of world civilisations in the era of globalisation.[35] He based his findings upon the radical religious fundamentalism and sometimes even violent and fanatic responses of the poor, the disadvantaged, the impoverished and the exploited nations to the increasing gap between the haves and have nots. These irreconcilable differences in the socio-economic, political, cultural and religious fronts seem to be accelerating at an unabating and alarming rate, despite increasing remedial efforts by the World Bank, the G8 and G12 nations, and the EEC.[36] With the 9/11 event in 2001, the Bali bombing massacre in 2002, the wars in Afghanistan in 2002 and Iraq in November 2003, one cannot but marvel at the accuracy of Huntington's prediction.

In the light of the increasing inter-connectedness in time and space through communication and technology, and a fragmentation of the relationship between nations and between the multi-cultural and pluralistic communities within nations, we need to be more proactive in rediscovering and reinventing ourselves in evangelicalism and the proclamation of the gospel.[37] In a collection of articles, evangelicals like Hutchinson have compiled a series of proposals about what remedial global approaches are needed to take evangelicalism into the era of globalisation.[38]

It is the aim of this essay to define certain strategic counter-measures to the negative impact of globalisation upon the proclamation of the gospel in the tiny nation of Vanuatu in the twenty-first century. In order to achieve a higher degree of compliance and reception to the proposed strategies, it shall be seen that one needs to have a proper understanding of the indigenous traditions and customs, their spiritual roots and belief systems, and of the socio-economic impact of globalisation. The rapid exposure to a democratic and Westernised form of government and bureaucracy over a course of twenty-five years (since Independence) has brought its inherent problems to this primarily tribal and agricultural society.[39]

These strategies will be outlined and discussed from a historical and local perspective and the methodology is specific and relevant in a Vanuatu context only.[40] Much of what the missionaries of the past 150 years experienced in this small emerging nation provides ample food for reflection as one attempts to formulate strategies towards an effective proclamation of the true gospel for a Vanuatu now challenged by the massive onslaught of globalisation in the twenty-first century.

Evangelicalism via a socio-political approach: The tribal chief system

As recently as 2002, Paramount Chief Claude Shem Masoerangi made the comment that in Vanuatu, the partnership between the chief and a pastor is as the two parts of an A-frame roof.[41] Indeed this is very true into the twenty-first century in Melanesian Vanuatu, where a large majority of the village chiefs have the dual roles of church leader (either as deacons or elders) and as village chief. It would be fair to say that if there is no working relationship between the church and the village chief, there will hardly be any proclamation of the gospel at all. Once the village chief refuses to welcome anyone into his territory, it is impossible to stay there with any degree of cooperation or satisfaction. Communal conversion is a common occurrence and one may wonder at times if there is any direct personal commitment at all to Christ. However no current statistics of the actual numbers involved are available.[42] Because of the pivotal role of the chief, it is essential to give primary consideration to this tribal chief system as one discerns strategies for the proclamation of the gospel in twenty-first-century Vanuatu.

Although Vanuatu is officially recognised by the United Nation as a free and democratically elected and independent sovereign nation consisting of some 83 islands, since its independence in July 1980, it is essential to understand that the majority of ni-Vanuatu still maintain an entrenched deep respect for their own particular tribal chief. In a primarily communal and agricultural setting, this may even take precedence over the elected national government of the day. When it comes to the implementation of policies of evangelistic outreach, the tribal chiefs would have an influential if not deciding impact upon the outcome. As most tribal chiefs and leaders are usually invited to be part of the official Government Advisory and Consultation process, most if not all differences and conflicts can be resolved before reaching a boiling point. In the case where irreconcilable differences exist between the tribal chiefs and elected government leaders, social unrest and disruption cannot be ruled out. The decisive role of these tribal chiefs and community leaders must be taken seriously in our formulation and implementation of strategies in the proclamation of the gospel. The fact that the first President of the State, Chief Ati George Sokomanlapa, and the first Prime Minister Father Walter Lini, and the planners for the independence of this new nation are all devoted Christians has much to say about their contributions in formulating sympathetic government policies towards the evangelisation by missionaries in the 1980s and 1990s.[43]

The chief has extensive power and authority over his constituents. He commands an unreserved respect and loyalty from them, even in this era of globalisation. Strictly speaking no one from his village can leave or enter his territory without his approval.[44] He will arbitrate on any disputes amongst his people and it is only when the matter cannot be resolved by him that it will be passed to the police or other law enforcement. He is frequently the judge and settles all matters of dispute and reconciliation in an impartial way. As the official of any ceremony, the chief's role is a fulltime responsibility. As a member of the National Council of Chiefs, he belongs to a selective group of leaders in the Vanuatu community and his authority runs through every fabric of the community under his rule. He even has the right to select the candidate to run for any Parliament election under his jurisdiction. As opposition parties are emerging, there is always an inherent and potential source of disunity for Vanuatu when the chief's power and authority is threatened. If the impartiality of the chief is transgressed through nepotism or corruption, his respect and loyalty will suffer accordingly.

Because of this prime role of the chiefs, they need to be adequately informed and equipped in evangelicalism. As the chiefly system is passed on to the first male on a hereditary basis, and wisdom is passed on from the father directly, it is important that appropriate evangelical measures and advice are available for their consideration. As they have profound influence upon the laws of the land, information on ethical issues from an evangelical point of view, such as human cloning and stem-cell research using human embryos, should be readily accessible to them. Although the National Council of Chiefs do provide updated information, and the local village chiefs do get together regularly to exchange information, it is still necessary for the global evangelical churches to be more proactive in providing sound biblical information and programs for these chiefs, so that these can be passed on to their constituents. Without their approval, it is difficult to filter any information down to the grass-root level. In this age of globalisation, the chiefs with any influence in the government of the day should be actively encouraged and lobbied to work closely with the existing churches. They should also be proactive in passing laws and setting guidelines for banning religious fundamentalism that promotes hatred and violence between religions groups, and banning religious cults that recommend civil disobedience and unacceptable civic traditions.

Evangelicalism via a socio-cultural approach: Inculturation and globalisation

On developing culturally appropriate strategies for the proclamation of the gospel in the twenty-first century, one must take note of sociologist Roland Robertson's proposals.[45] He argued well that 'religious factors will almost certainly be intimately involved in those variegated strategies for relating individuals and national societies to the emerging global order'.[46] Robertson envisaged globalisation as making the key features of modernity global. According to Robertson, it would be just a matter of time before any recent advances in technology, science and communication will filter down into the local villages. Globalisation has fast tracked this process into a fine art. In his analysis of global-ity, Robertson proposes four successive levels of influence: the individual, the nation-state, the inter-societal, and humanity. It is therefore not surprising for him to suggest that in the global age, religion should be expected to play an even more relevant and assertive role than just at the individual level. Garrett was correct to draw our attention to Robertson's suggestion that religion must not be marginalised nor secularised to the private concern of individuals only. In a globalised world, what one does can have consequences upon the whole world. In summary it is fair to say that religion and culture are intimately intertwined in a global world and one cannot dissociate the two in formulating any strategies on evangelicalism.

Globalisation brings a global contextualisation of cultures. This leads to an on-going crisis of identity, as in the case of the ni-Vanuatu. As a result of the rise in nationalism since its independence, religious leaders and the chiefs alike have been at pains to inculturate Christianity with their religious beliefs and customs. Through adoption and accommodation, Christianity was made more palatable to the indigenous people. An example of the globalisation of Christianity and traditional beliefs would be in the ceremonial sacrifices of pigs to appease their traditional gods and in reconciliation ceremonies. This has now been given a new twist and interpreted as similar to sacrifices in the Old Testament times, and Jesus is the once and for all final sacrifice.[47] In the case of bride-price, it has been a matter of 'accommodation'. Bride-price is a tradition where the young boy's parents choose a bride for their son and a price is given as down payment until the girl is old enough for marriage. The amount involved is in terms of a number of pigs, and other food and material is set, according to one's status and wealth.

This is an entrenched custom in Vanuatu and early missionaries, instead of abolishing it and antagonising every one in the village, compromised by setting a limit as to how much the bride-price would be. Even this was opposed at various levels, but the antagonism to abolishing the practice completely would have been even worse. Some indigenous church leaders have even rationalised the bride-price practice as biblical, as it cost the man Adam a rib from his side to create his wife![48] It can therefore be illustrated that evangelical missionaries are often seen as the key interpreters of non-Western societies to the West and vice versa.

For evangelicalism to be more compliable in twenty-first-century Vanuatu, indigenous pastors, church leaders and village chiefs should work together with missionaries from the global village to maintain the forum in dealing with such issues on traditions and customs. With the risk of syncretism and compromising the gospel, this is even more important in this global age. The Gospel and Culture in Vanuatu Ministry, as initiated by Randall Prior, is a means for such and should be actively encouraged.

Evangelicalism via the Word: Theological education

The important role of a sound theological education in the era of globalisation cannot be underestimated. Robertson regarded the period 1875 to 1925 as the 'take off' phase of globalisation and suggested Western capitalism and Christian missionaries played important roles in creating Western education systems in nations that had previously been unknown to them. They not only provided basic knowledge in science and technology, but also biblical moral principles and guidelines for the developing nations. Many non-Western leaders were educated in the West.[49] Missionaries such as John Geddie and Bishop Selwyn, in their evangelical works in Vanuatu in the nineteenth century, would be good cases in point. The importance of theological education in the era of globalisation is also supported by others, including Stackhouse. He maintained that 'globalisation will further enhance and has a decisive role in theological education as the evangelicals strive for an evangelisation of the world with a greater theological and socio-analytical integrity'.[50] Of course theological education refers to the understanding of the truth as revealed by the Bible. Bockmuehl gave the example of English-speaking evangelicals who became missionary-minded when the German Pietist Movement returned to the Bible and had a renewed appreciation and understanding of the Great Commission (Matthew 28:16–20).[51] Prior to this, according to Bockmuehl, the call to discipleship as understood by Luther and

Calvin had been a spiritual call to the ministry as a profession rather than a call to 'make disciples of all nations'. This revival in the understanding of the Word led to the subsequent growth of the cross-cultural missions.

If theological education is of such importance, how then might we formulate strategies in twenty-first-century Vanuatu? This is a country where the national illiteracy rate is close to 53 percent and with 60 percent of the population under the age of 16 years. It is a small nation with only 220,000 ni-Vanuatu, where communication and didactic teaching are oral rather than by written tradition, and on top of that at least 100 different languages used. Transport and energy resources are scarce and expensive and limited to the only two large urban centres, Port Vila and Luganville. This is largely the result of the socio-economic impoverishment caused by globalisation. As mentioned, the tribal chief system and a strong church polity set up by the Presbyterian Church and the Church of Melanesia since the nineteenth century provided the answer.[52] Since the 1840s, the evangelicals Bishop Selwyn of the Anglican Church and John Geddie of the Church of Scotland divided the then New Hebrides into two regions as far as evangelicalism is concerned, the islands to the north (including the Banks range of Islands) being primarily the Anglican's concern and the southern islands, Presbyterian. They had a mutual understanding of the evangelistic task ahead and the agreement still holds today. The Vanuatu Council of Churches was later formed as more churches joined as a coherent unit for reaching out to the ni-Vanuatu; these are churches that subscribe to the belief in a triune God.[53]

Through globalisation and this network of evangelical churches, and in cooperation with the National Council of Chiefs, a whole range of comprehensive programs are in place. Such programs include the Wycliffe Bible Translators, who do not only have to learn the local language and then to translate this and record it in written form, but also have the laborious task of teaching the people how to read the Bible in their own language. The Bible Society provides agents for the printing and distribution of Bislama Bibles, while language recordings, songs and drama are being broadcast to the Pacific Rim from Asia via satellites (local communities use solar-powered receivers to turn into Christian programs). Leadership training and updated information regarding cultic activities can be readily accessed in this age of globalisation.

Perhaps the most significant of all developments is the founding of the Talua Ministry Training Centre in Santo for the education of future church leaders and pastors, because a healthy church depends upon a proper understanding of the Word. It is encouraging to know that the evangelical members of the Vanuatu Council of Churches are united in evangelicalism by sending their best available students, teachers and resources for the training of these future church leaders. Although they are constantly out of resources due to the unending demand for better and more church leaders, the centre at Talua has received support from overseas churches and mission organisations.

Evangelicalism via more effective witnessing: Missions

Views are circulating that certain conversions in Vanuatu are communal conversions, whilst others are for reasons of wealth and material gain, and syncretism is also a problem in the proclamation of the gospel.[54] On occasions a whole village is converted to Christ based on the decision of the tribal chief. The entire village may follow the village chief without each person having a personal commitment to Christ as Lord and Saviour. Others would see conversion to Christ as offering a more comfortable earthly life or financial reward. Syncretism of traditional beliefs and customs with Christianity has always been a danger. Although it is difficult to ascertain the extent of these occurrences, we need to address these issues nonetheless and the sooner the better.

One of the ways to deal with this in the age of globalisation is to increase the exposure of the people to the Christian lifestyle. Mere theological training for church leaders and the chiefs may not be enough. Because of the relative ease and convenience in travelling between Vanuatu and the neighbouring developed nations, missionaries and short-term missions can facilitate their exposure to what being a Christian means. As most ni-Vanuatu are illiterate, evangelistic programs via music, drama and games may be more appropriate. Not only can the gospel be re-enacted, but Christian moral values can also be instilled at the same time. Via the network of missionaries, models of prayer and worship can be introduced. As their intellectual knowledge of God's love in Christ can be displayed via dramas and songs and on a repeated basis from multiple witnesses, evangelicalism can be achieved via catechesis, edification and discernment.[55] The inclusion of the recital of the Apostles' Creed, and its explanation, in the worship service would help to clarify the meaning of the triune Christian God. Edification is via the use of one's spiritual gifts in building up one another in Christ. In a global context, the traffic can be both ways, with Christians from Vanuatu and abroad on regular cultural exchanges organised and sponsored by wealthier churches and mission organisations in the global village.

Evangelicalisation is more than just an imparting of biblical knowledge, it is also exposing the way the Christian truths are applied to human lives. Ni-Vanuatu are basically an urban and agricultural society, and globalisation has further alienated them from the benefits of modernisation. Short-term missions and exchange programs for Christian family ministry can be introduced. Workshops for parenting in a Vanuatu context can also be instituted through the help of lay Christians in developed nations. There is an increasing trend of baby boomers going into early retirement. Perhaps the lay Christians amongst this age bracket can be mobilised for more active involvement in conducting these worthwhile ministries in Vanuatu.[56] This catechesis, edification and discernment is not an end in itself. The goal is never-ending and involves an on-going process of witness to Christ so that people can be more Christ-like.

Although Vanuatu is an impoverished nation requiring considerable aid from friendly nations and the United Nations, project-orientated aid is preferable to direct financial aid. Although it may be mistakenly interpreted as intrusion into one's internal affairs at times, it seems to be the best way to get assistance to the areas where aid is needed most. Lack of reliable human resources on a regular basis appears to be the problem and this may be addressed with socio-economic aid or with financing Christian programs.

Evangelicalism via socio-economic reforms: Cultural exchanges and foreign aid

It would be incomplete if one were to ignore the socio-economic dimension of evangelicalism. The cults are adept at 'bribing' their way into the Vanuatu communities with education and health services.[57] Kindergarten and primary schools, medical and dental health clinics, hospitals, direct financial aid to community projects, promotions via glossy printings and free handouts and leaflets, certainly have their impact on the ni-Vanuatu people. If the religious fringe groups can be so assertive and successful in their promotion, it is a puzzle why evangelicals cannot match this with a similar degree of enthusiasm.

In the South Pacific Forum in Samoa in August 2004, the Prime Minister of Australia, John Howard, noted that direct financial aid may not be the best available option to help the South Pacific nations reeling under the crushing impact of globalisation.[58] He suggested that there are five areas needing to be addressed. One would be wise therefore, to take note of these in formulating strategies for the effective proclamation of the gospel.

Corruption and nepotism amongst certain Pacific nation leaders are rife and proper accountability has been a recurrent issue. This is not only at government level, but even involves evangelical churches![59] There is also an inability to cope with the massive scale of administration and rapid changes in the areas of communication and technology. Proper management and wastage of natural and human resources were also noted to be important factors. These resulted in further exploitation by certain multinationals and criminal elements. As a consequence, socio-economic aid for the purpose of proclamation of the gospel is better offered on a project-orientated basis than in monetary forms. And there is much the evangelical churches both abroad and in Vanuatu can imitate from the projects supported by the cultic groups in Vanuatu which, alas, have achieved a certain degree of success.

Conclusion

Vanuatu is only a young and small Melanesian nation in the Pacific Basin, gaining national independence at the time when globalisation was on the rise. The negative impact of globalisation is tremendous upon these primarily agricultural tribal communities of 83 islands. Generally ignored by large mission organisations, twenty-first-century Vanuatu is the focus of increasing proselytising activities from certain Western cults and foreign religions. This essay has highlighted some of the important areas requiring consideration as one formulates strategies for evangelicalism. The proposal is for a multiple disciplinary approach with a clear understanding of traditional cultural and religious beliefs and through the existing joint cooperation of the leaders and chiefs of the Vanuatu Council of Churches, the National Council of Chiefs, and the elected Vanuatu government of the day.

Bibliography

Armstrong, E. S., *The Melanesian Mission*, London: Isbister, 1900

Beckwith, R. T. & Selman, M. J., *Sacrifices in the Bible*, London: publisher, 1995

Bosch, D. J., *Transforming Mission: Paradigm Shifts in Theology of Mission*, Maryknoll, NY: Orbis, 2002

Engel, J. & Dyrness, W., *Changing the Mind of Missions: Where Have We Gone Wrong?*, Grand Rapids: IVP, 2000

Friedman, T. L., *The Lexus and the Olive Tree: Understanding Globalisation*, Farrar, Strauss: Giroux, 1999

Garrett, J., *To Live Among the Stars*, Geneva: WCC Publishers, 1982

Garrett, W. R., 'Thinking Religion in the Global Circumstances: A Critique of Roland Robertson's Globalization Theory', *Journal for the Scientific Study of Religion*, 31 (1992)

Gillian, H. R., *Vanuatu Victory: Four Generations of Sharing Christian Faith in the Pacific*, Warburton, Victoria: Spectrum, 1988

Hillard, D., *God's Gentlemen: A History of the Melanesian Mission 1849–1942*, Brisbane: University of Queensland Press, 1978

Hutchinson, M. & Kalu, O., *A Global Faith: Essays on Evangelism and Globalization*, Sydney: Openbook, 1998

Huntington, S. P., *The Clash of Civilizations and the Remaking of World Order*, Place: Touchstone, 1996

Jenkins, P., *The Next Christendom: The Coming of Global Christianity*, London: Oxford University Press, 2002

Miller, J. G., *Live Book 1*, Sydney: Presbyterian Church of Australia, 2001

Newbigin, L., *Foolishness to the Greeks: The Gospel and Western Culture*, Grand Rapids: Eerdmans, 1986

Newbigin, L., *The Gospel in a Pluralist Society*, Grand Rapids: Eerdmans, 1989

O'Byrne & Harcombe, *Vanuatu*, 3rd edition, Melbourne: Lonely Planet Publications, 1999

Prior, R., *World Council of Churches Study Process on Gospel and Cultures*, Santo, Vanuatu: Talua Ministry Training Centre, 1995

Prior, R., *Gospel and Culture in Vanuatu: The Founding Missionary and a Missionary for Today*, Melbourne: Gospel Vanuatu Books, 1998

Prior, R., editor, *Gospel and Culture in Vanuatu 2: Contemporary Local Perspectives*, Melbourne: Gospel Vanuatu Books, 2001

Prior, R., editor, *Gospel and Culture in Vanuatu 3: The Voice of the Local Church*, Melbourne: Gospel Vanuatu Books, 2003

Ramachandra, V., *Gods That Fail: Modern Idolatry and Christian Mission*, Grand Rapids: IVP, 1996

Robertson, R., 'Globalization and Societal Movements', *American Anthropologist*, Vol. 58 (1956)

Smith, D., *Mission after Christendom*, London: DLT, 2003

Stackhouse, M. L., 'The Global Future and the Future of Globalisation', *Christian Century*, 2–9 February 1994

Stackhouse, M. L. & Browning, D. S., *God and Globalization: The Spirit and the Modern Authorities*, Vol. 2, Harrisburg: Trinity Press International, 2001

Taylor, J. V., *The Scattered Self*, London: The Prime Vision, 1963

Taylor, W. D., editor, *Global Missiology for the 21st Century: The Iguassu Dialogue*, Grand Rapids: Baker, 2000

Tiplady, R., editor, *One World or Many: The Impact of Globalisation on Missions*, Pasadena: William Carey Library, 2003

Tiplady, R., editor, *Postmission: Mission by a Post-Modern Generation*, Place: Paternoster, 2003

Tippett, A. R., *The Deep Sea Canoe Stories of the Spread of the Gospel by South Pacific Island Missionaries*, Wewak, PNG: Wirui Press, 1994

Trompf, G., editor, *The Gospel is Not Western*, Maryknoll, NY: Orbis, 1987

Walls, A. E., *The Missionary Movement in Christian History: Studies in the Transmission of Faith*, Melbourne: Orbis, 1997

Webber, R. E., *Ancient-Future Faith: Rethinking Evangelicalism for a Postmodern World*, Grand Rapids: Baker Books, 1999

Webber, R. E., *The Younger Evangelicals: Facing the Challenges of the New World*, Grand Rapids: Baker, 2002

Whiteman, D., *An Introduction to Melanesian Cultures*, Goroka, PNG: Melanesian Institute, 1984

Wright, C. & Fugui, L., editors, *Christ in South Pacific Cultures*, Suva, Fuji: Lotu Pasifica, 1985

Van Der Veer, P., *Conversion to Modernities: The Globalisation of Modernity*, London: Routledge, 1996

Verstraelen, F. J., editor, *Missiology: An Ecumenical Introduction Texts and contents of Global Christianity*, Grand Rapids: Eerdmans, 1995

God's Forgiveness and
Its Cultural Implications

John Riches

In thinking about this topic we must be careful to distinguish between two different aspects of forgiveness: (1) God's forgiveness of our sin, and (2) Our forgiveness of others. God's forgiveness should be seen as an example and pattern for the type of forgiveness we are expected to extend to others, but there are also some important differences.

I invite you to consider the following questions in relation to our forgiveness of others. As a Christian:

1 Whom must I forgive?
2 What things (actions) must I forgive?
3 How often must I forgive?
4 Why must I forgive?
5 What is the effect (result) of forgiveness?
6 What part does confession play in forgiveness?
7 What part does repentance play in forgiveness?
8 What part does restitution play in forgiveness?
9 What part does reconciliation play in forgiveness?
10 What part should the church play in forgiveness?

Historical (biblical) background

Human understanding of God's requirements of his people in regard to forgiveness (and its opposite, revenge) has changed throughout history as God has progressively revealed his character and his will. Some biblical texts will provide a quick overview:

[Insert Table]

Let us now look at some Bible verses that can help us to answer the introductory questions.

1. Whom must I forgive?

In order to answer this question we must consider what is meant by the term 'forgive'. There are various possible ways to understand what forgiveness involves.

Firstly, forgiveness means abandoning all anger, resentment and bitterness that I may have in my heart toward someone who has wronged me. This is probably the type of forgiveness meant in Mark

11:25, which says, 'When you stand praying, if you hold anything against anyone, forgive him, so that your Father in heaven may forgive you your sins'. Scripture also gives two further reasons why we must be prepared to do this: I should see the wrong action as defiance of God, rather than an action against me personally (see Psalm 51:4); and carrying resentment and anger in my heart will achieve no good purpose, but will only harm myself and prevent me from serving God as I should (James 1:20; Proverbs 29:11; 30:33). However, true forgiveness is more than just failure to seek revenge or administer punishment.

Secondly, forgiveness means completely forgetting the wrong that has been done and continuing from that time on as if it had never happened. This is the type of forgiveness God offers to those who turn away from their sin and come to God in repentance.

An important difference between these two types of forgiveness should be clearly understood: the first type involves only the person who has been wronged, whether the sinner is repentant or not; but the second type must always be conditional on true repentance and, where possible, also requires restitution (compare 1 John 1:9 and Luke 17:3 with Luke 19:8).

2. What things (actions) must I forgive?

We have already seen that we should not carry anger and resentment in our hearts toward those who have wronged us, but true forgiveness (the second type explained above), like God's forgiveness of our sins, should always be conditional on the other person confessing, repenting and doing as much as he can to put things right (restitution). To simply overlook and forget about a sin without these things being present would be inviting further trouble, both from the same person and from others. It would ignore the fact that all sin is a serious offence against God's law that cannot be lightly dismissed – in fact, it can only be forgiven (when the conditions are fulfilled) because Christ died on the cross to pay the price of our redemption. It is necessary to understand, and to teach others (including those who wrong us) that all sin must be punished (see Roman 6:23 where the 'wages' are not just an entitlement, but an automatic and unavoidable result of sin).

Either we accept that Christ has borne the punishment for us, or we must bear it ourselves. Even when there has been true repentance and forgiveness, it must be recognised that in this world a sin will often have continuing and lasting consequences. Biblical examples include Moses (Deuteronomy 3:25–26), Eli (1 Samuel 3:14), and David (2 Samuel 12:13–14).

Another type of wrong (or sinful action) needs to be mentioned – sins that the person doing them is unaware of because he lacks understanding or genuinely does not see them as wrong. Such ignorance can never excuse the sin. An action contrary to God's will is a sin whether we are aware of it or not. In Psalm 19:12 David recognises that such acts are sins for which he needs to ask God's forgiveness. But how can I confess a sin when I am not aware that it is a sin? First, like David I can confess in general that because I am a sinner I accept that there will be such sins in my life, and ask for God's forgiveness. Secondly, I can take comfort from the fact that such sins can be forgiven without the need for specific confession and repentance. However this can only happen because such sins are covered by Christ's sacrifice and he has borne the punishment for them. The only sins that are not covered by Christ's sacrifice are those we wilfully bear responsibility for ourselves because we insist that there is nothing wrong in what we have done, and we are not prepared to turn away from doing it. In such cases we are not penitent and ignore or reject the work of the Holy Spirit who convicts us – this is the 'unpardonable sin' mentioned in Matthew 12:31.

3. How often must I forgive?

The number 490 mentioned by Jesus in Matthew 18:22 is obviously not to be taken as a specific numerical limit. We are not to keep count, but to continue forgiving just as God does when there is true repentance. If we are not prepared to forgive others, how can we expect God to forgive us? (See also Matthew 6:12 and Colossians 3:13).

4. Why must I forgive?

The answer to this question is simple: we must be prepared to forgive others who sin against us because God has forgiven us for our sin against God. Jesus made this point unforgettably by telling his followers the parable of the Unforgiving Servant. In Matthew 18:23–35, Jesus makes it very clear that anyone who refuses to forgive his fellow man is placing himself in the same position as the servant who had been forgiven an enormous debt by the king, but refused to forgive his fellow-servant even a very small debt.

5. What is the effect (result) of forgiveness?

We have seen already that even after my sin has been forgiven (by God, or by a person whom I have wronged), there may be lasting effects. The damage done to someone else cannot always be undone. Simple justice may require that the sin cannot be forgotten and dismissed from our minds. There may be a continuing price that has to be paid. Obvious examples are murder and children born out of wedlock as a result of rape, adultery or fornication.

6. What part does confession play in forgiveness?

Confession is necessary before forgiveness can take place. It is a prerequisite for repentance. If I will not admit that I have done something wrong, how can I be truly repentant? In 1 John 1:9, the apostle John makes clear that God will forgive our sins if we confess our sins. But this statement must be qualified by the truth taught in other parts of God's word. Two further points need to be noted. Firstly, unconfessed sin can also be forgiven in some situations, for example, when the sin is committed unknowingly – see under the answer to question 2 above. Secondly, Jesus prayed on the cross, 'Father, forgive them, for they do not know what they are doing' (Luke 23:34). The Roman soldiers who crucified Jesus were merely obeying orders from their commander, and this clearly tells us that their unawareness of the sin they were committing, while in no way lessening the guilt attached to the sin, was a reason why they could be forgiven by the Father. A person who is innocent of any sin cannot be forgiven. The fact that Christ asked the Father to forgive them means that they were guilty. And we cannot imagine that Christ would have been asking the Father to do what is impossible – unknown sin can be forgiven by God without having to be confessed and repented of, because of Christ's sacrifice. The necessity of Christ's sacrifice must be emphasised whenever this truth is expounded, as there is no way to come to the Father except through Christ and what he has done (John 14:6).

This important principle has implications for the possible forgiveness of infants or insane adults who lack understanding of what they are doing, as well as for people who are unaware of sin because they have never heard the gospel. However, we do not have space here to consider such things in greater detail. Some other relevant biblical texts are Romans 2:14–16, Matthew 16:27 and Genesis 18:25.

7. What part does repentance play in forgiveness?

As we have seen, repentance is essential before there can be any true forgiveness. But repentance is more than just wishing you had not committed the sin and feeling sorry for its consequences. That can be described as remorse, but it is not true repentance. One interesting definition of repentance is found in Ezekiel 6:9, which says, 'they will loathe themselves for the evil they have done'. A truly repentant sinner is determined to turn away from the sin because he understands that he has defied God; he knows that his sin caused the death of God's Son, and he cannot bear the thought of doing such a thing again.

This raises the question of how we can tell whether or not someone who has wronged us has truly repented of their sin and should be forgiven. Should we be making such judgments in the light of verses such as Matthew 7:1 ('Do not judge, or you too will be judged')? In most situations of one person sinning against another, there may not be any need to make such a judgment, because the administration of justice is not within our powers and responsibilities. However, as we shall see below, the making of such judgments cannot be avoided by governments, churches and even parents. In many situations we cannot simply accept the word of the sinner that they have repented; there must be convincing evidence that the person has indeed turned away from the sin and will not continue to sin in that way.

8. What part does restitution play in forgiveness?

Restitution (or recompense or restoration) is often desirable (as in the example of Zacchaeus), and sometimes necessary, but will not always be possible; and even if it is possible it may not be a satisfactory answer. The Old Testament's 'eye for an eye and tooth for a tooth' principle was always intended as a limit on revenge, not an invariable right to compensation. Thus, if I commit adultery with your wife, I cannot make restitution by giving you my wife for a night, and if you kill one of my children I cannot make it right by killing one of your children. But if I steal, kill and eat one of your bullocks, then in addition to my repentance, justice requires that I at least give you a bullock in return before I can expect to be forgiven.

9. What part does reconciliation play in forgiveness?

Reconciliation should follow forgiveness when one person has sinned against another and has truly repented of their sin. But it cannot bring about forgiveness. No action that person can perform will result in their sin being forgiven by God, nor can it result in their sin against another person being forgiven by that person. Only true repentance can result in forgiveness.

10. What part should the church play in forgiveness?

The church, and each individual Christian, has a ministry of reconciliation. The first priority is to bring about reconciliation between humanity and God (2 Corinthians 5:18), but the making of peace between humans who have set themselves against each other is also an important ministry of the church (Matthew 5:9).

Forgiveness and Vanuatu cultures

As an ex-patriate, I have limited understanding of the ni-Vanuatu culture and traditional ceremonies, so I can only make a few general comments about the way reconciliation is used and viewed in Vanuatu, and my comments will have to be based on the biblical truths explained above. Here I must make a very important point: scriptural teaching and truth applies to all cultures. If our cultural traditions and practices are contrary to the teaching of God's word, then we must change the culture; we cannot change God's word to make it fit in with our cultural practices. Some people make the mistake of thinking that biblical truth has some direct connection with Western or European culture. In fact, it was given to people with a Jewish culture, but the writers of the New Testament made clear that it applied equally to people in other cultures, such as the Greeks, Romans and Egyptians. You must decide for yourself how well your cultural traditions fit in with the truth contained in God's word.

- The church should always be seeking to promote peace and reconciliation between individual men and women, families, clans, tribes, villages, and so on.
- Reconciliation has little meaning or relevance unless there is true repentance by anyone and everyone who has done wrong.
- The killing of pigs or exchanging of other gifts can be a useful symbol, but should never be seen or accepted as a means of 'buying' forgiveness.
- Repentance must be accompanied by convincing evidence of a changed heart and life, and this evidence can only be given over a period of time.
- The church is responsible for exercising discipline among its members and leaders. Sins cannot be simply overlooked, whether repented of or not. Justice must be seen to be done whenever possible, so that both church members and outsiders can see that the church views sin seriously.
- In conflict situations, the church must not take the easy way out by assuming that there is fault equally on both sides. That is seldom the case, and to act on such an assumption would be unjust. Matters must be fully investigated, sin must be exposed (compare 'show him his fault', Matthew 18:15), and sinners must accept responsibility for what they have done.
- Reconciliation must not be used as a means of avoiding justice that may require restitution, compensation, or imprisonment in order to ensure the safety of the community and provide a deterrent to other possible offenders. This applies in the church as well as in civil matters.
- Sins that have been repented and forgiven must still be taken into account in future dealings with the sinner. The church has a responsibility to help the sinner to avoid further sins of the same type.
- A leader (such as pastor, priest, elder, youth leader, Sunday school teacher) must always be 'above reproach' and set a good example. If he or his wife commits one of the sins mentioned in 1 Timothy 3:2–12, then he no longer fulfils the scriptural requirements for holding a position of leadership in the church, and he must resign his position or have it taken from him. These sins include intemperance (for example, drunkenness), sexual immorality, lack of self-control,

violence, inability to control his own children, dishonesty and gossiping.
• The church cannot simply overlook sin without exercising effective discipline. Neither can a parent or government. Imagine the result if all criminals were simply forgiven instead of being punished. Even when the offender is truly repentant and we are certain that he will not re-offend, it would be an open invitation for others to commit similar crimes. Church discipline must be seen and handled in the same way. We must remember that when God forgives our sin, the sin is not merely cancelled or overlooked. Justice must be done and punishment must be borne – but praise God! Instead of us having to bear the punishment ourselves, it is borne by God's own Son who died in our place.

Conclusion

The church cannot be seen to support any ceremony that involves or implies that forgiveness is being 'purchased' by the giving of gifts or by the sacrifice of an animal, or could be understood as meaning that the sin is being overlooked. The church should have no part in supporting or accepting any type of 'reconciliation ceremony' unless it includes the following: admission of guilt, confession of sin, evidence of true repentance, restitution (to whatever extent is possible), punishment (where appropriate), and recognition of continuing effects (if applicable).

If sin can be forgiven and its effects nullified by performing a ceremony which does not involve these things, then the message it proclaims is that there was no need for Christ to come into the world and die on the cross.

Bibliography

Arnold, Clinton E., The Colossian Syncretism, Grand Rapids: Baker Books, 1996

Mantovani, Ennio, 'What is Religion?', in *An Introduction to Melanesian Religions*, Point No. 6, Goroka Melanesian Institute, 1968

McDonald, Mary, 'Symbolism and Myth', in *An Introduction to Melanesian Religions*, Point No. 6, 1968

Tillich, Paul., *Theology of Culture*, London: Oxford University Press, 1972

Whiteman, Darrell, 'Melanesian Religions: An Overview', in *An Introduction to Melanesian Religions*, Point No. 6, Goroka Melanesian Institute, 1968

Contextualisation: A Journey from Colossae to Melanesia

Bruce Nicholls

Introduction

I have chosen as our context Melanesia rather than Vanuatu, Papua New Guinea, the Solomon Islands or Fiji for three reasons. First, my personal experience in the region is very limited. Second, the plurality and diversity of languages and cultures in the region suggests that this essay can do no more than discern some general characteristics of the region. Third, while traditional religions and cultures continue to be the bedrock of Melanesian society, changes are beginning to escalate. With the coming of Christianity 150 years ago, traditional religions have been largely replaced by the Christian religion with its overlay of Western culture. The majority of people in Melanesia call themselves Christians with perhaps only five to ten percent retaining their traditional beliefs and practices – often in opposition to Christianity. The impact of a secular technological culture through radio, television, trade and travel is changing the culture. I sense that during the next fifty years Melanesia will experience even more radical changes, especially as China tightens her grip on the economy of the South Pacific, and Islam penetrates every nation in the region with a radically new religious culture. The history of Indonesia points to what could happen in the South Pacific. The plan of this essay is to:

1 Survey the general pattern and characteristics of traditional religions and cultures in Melanesia.
2 Outline the reasons for the crisis in the church at Colossae and Paul's response to it.
3 Suggest the significance of this issue for the churches in Melanesia today and during the coming decades.

General patterns of traditional religions and cultures in Melanesia

Religion and culture can be distinguished but not separated. In the words of Paul Tillich, 'Religion is the substance of culture, culture is the form of religion' (Tillich, p. 42). Every religious act is culturally contained. While culture is the total way of life of a given community, including customs, social institutions, values and ideological worldviews, religion is its chief characteristic and motivating power for action. This is true for Melanesian culture (and even more so for Islam). The distinctive characteristic of any culture is the shape of its coherence and comprehensiveness in belief and practice.

The ultimate dynamics and ethos of Melanesian culture are its concern for the continuity of life in the present. The ancestors, though dead, are living members of the present clan or community.

Religion is not merely a human construct, but the encounter between the transcendent that Christians define as God and the people in their search for harmony and life. It is a divine–human encounter. Ennio Mantovani of the Melanesian Institute at Goroka, Papua New Guinea, characterises religion as either theistic or biocosmic (Mantovani, p. 31). By 'theistic' he includes those whose religious experience is to trust in a transcendent Creator who is lawgiver, father, friend and Lord of all things. The three great monotheistic religions – Judaism, Christianity and Islam – belong in this category. By 'biocosmic', Mantovani means the religious experience of those whose focus is the reality called 'life' (*bios*) lived out in the cosmic realm of personal existence, health, well-being, wealth and harmony of relationships, seen and unseen. It is the ordered inter-relatedness with the environment and people in the community. It is material, biological and spiritual – a horizontal orientation. Traditional Melanesian religion belongs to the biocosmic experience.

The Melanesian worldview includes both the empirical that can be seen and touched – the natural environment, animals and people – and the non-empirical – the world of spirits, ghosts and the living dead. Together they form one cosmos, one present reality. The spirit world is often perceived in human form. The spirits are 'part of both local space and time. They are here and now, intermingling with the empirical world of people and the natural environment' (Whiteman, p. 89). The concept of *mana* first discussed in Melanesia by the New Zealand Anglican missionary Robert Codrington in 1891 is the power or life-force manifest in the leadership gifts of individuals. It reflects an important element in Melanesian religion to which the Hebrew *shalom* comes close, Whiteman suggests, captivating the essence of salvation in Melanesia. Salvation is success in all aspects of human life (Whiteman, p. 101).

Rituals

Rituals have an important place in Melanesian religion, holding together the communal responses to harvesting a garden, healing a sick child, entering into marriage, coping with death, and experiencing the power or *mana* of the unseen life-force. Rituals are also important for cyclic festivals associated with the regular changes of the solar and lunar calendar, such as planting and harvesting of the taro and other crops. Some Christians interpret these rituals as idolatrous as they are directed to the spirit world and they believe they must be abandoned. But this is not necessarily so. It depends on where the power comes from in the success of the ritual – from God in Christ or from the spirits. This issue has become a matter of hot debate in the Melanesian churches. If the power is other than God and if trust in Christ to save and to act is weakened, then it is idolatrous. The ritual is only the means to the stated goal.

Ennio Mantovani discusses the case of the ritual of healing. If the purpose of the ritual is to obtain help from the spirits and powers that are not gods, then it is wrong and could be classified as magic. But in the biocosmic thought system, if the worshipper is trusting only in the power of the nature medicine to heal, then the ritual may be acceptable. The question is not which ritual is valid, but whether the ritual is seen as an end in itself or as an instrument of healing that God uses to God's glory. This applies to modern Western medicine as well. Its use is also a ritual. It is a question of where we put our faith. Is the purpose of the ritual of healing in the biocosmic world to establish good relationships with the spirit world or with God the Creator as a pre-condition to healing? It is not how the healing occurs, but who heals. In the biblical history, faith in God or in the name of Jesus Christ was the pre-condition to healing. In the case of Naaman, he was asked to wash in the river Jordan seven times. James calls for the ritual of anointing with oil and the laying-on of hands. These are also rituals.

Secrecy

Secrecy is an important element in Melanesian religion as it is in most religions. Secrecy ensures the possession of power of the one initiated. In Hindu transcendental meditation, the giving of a secret *mantra* or name by the guru will ensure the release of power. In the Old Testament the name Yahweh was never pronounced. He is always *adonai*, 'the Lord'. But in the New Testament the mystery of God is 'now disclosed to all the saints' (Colossians 1:26). The mystery is 'Christ in you the hope of glory'. The power of the gospel lies in it being an open secret.

Ancestors

Ancestors hold a central place in Melanesian religion, though their importance varies throughout Melanesia. In Vanuatu their place is less important than it is in New Guinea (Whiteman, p. 105). If the ancestor was a great warrior or a gardener, his power or *mana* increased with his death. His spirit or ghost can bring great blessing or sickness and death to the clan. Though dead, he is a living member of the family. In time, these historical ancestors may take on the attributes of mythological ancestors known collectively as *dema* deities. The violent death of a *dema* ancestor may bring the blessings of prosperity to the whole clan. The evangelist sympathetic to his culture may see in this myth a bridge to preach the meaning of the Cross. At the same time, Melanesian people trust the spirits who inhabit the tops of mountains or particular trees to bring blessing. Then there are creator deities as in most primal religions, who are generally remote from the life of the community, but do point to an ultimate Creator.

Myths

Myths, as with rituals, are symbols of reality. Rituals are expressed in dramatic forms, while myths are stories that enhance the values of a culture. Mary McDonald, a Catholic missionary sister working in New Guinea, tells children a story explaining why possums live in the forest and dogs in the village. In the story, they lived together in the men's long-house. Then they quarrelled over the way they ate food. During a heated discussion, the dog chased the possum into the bush. Because the rift was never healed, dogs continue to hunt possums (McDonald). Myths are 'media of religious experience and insights'.

The search for identity

During the past twenty years, the nations of Melanesia have drunk deeply from the wells of liberation from colonial rule. But they continue to struggle to define their identity as people being threatened by new forms of colonisation. In the search for dignity and nationhood there is a renewal of interest in their traditional religions and culture (as there is with the Maori of New Zealand). Though the people are virtually all Christian, even if nominally so, the churches are seeking to define the boundaries between the true contextualising of their faith in the context of their traditional cultures and the syncretistic tendencies to absorb pagan values and worldviews into their Christian faith.

The danger is that they might lose the reality of their faith in Christ by so doing. The issue of the relationship of identity in Christ and in one's culture is a global one, not only for the developing world, but also for the Christian West as well. The church in Melanesia is not the first church to experience this crisis. The great theological centres of Alexandria and Antioch faced similar challenges in the first century of the church. The formulating of the ecumenical creeds that followed was an attempt to break the 'Latin captivity of the church'. They were only partially successful. Similarly, in Asia and the South Pacific, the struggle for the church's identity will be a long one.

Contextualisation and syncretism in Colossae

We now turn to the church in Colossae in the years AD 55–62 as Paul faced dissension in the church, and discover how he dealt with it. Colossae was a small town in the Lycus Valley of Asia Minor (now Turkey), 180 kilometres east of Ephesus. It was the centre of a farming community famous for its woollen industry. It has been my privilege to stand on the high mound of the unexcavated town and look down the valley to the ruins of Laodicea and across the valley to Hieropolis with its steaming white terraces. It was a tourist centre famous for its mineral baths and its pagan temples. Paul refers to these towns in his letter to the church. The church at Colossae was founded by Epaphras who had been converted when Paul was preaching in Ephesus for two years between AD 52 and 55. Epaphras returned home to plant churches in the towns of this rich agricultural valley. The church in Colossae comprised one or more house churches, one of which was in the home of Philemon, a slave owner. Some five to seven years later, Paul was in prison, most probably in Rome. Tychicus went to Rome with good news of the church, but also the disturbing news of dissension within its members. Paul responded by sending a letter with Tychicus to the faithful church members in Colossae. He also sent a more personal but open letter to Philemon appealing to him to accept his slave Onesimus back as a brother in Christ.

As always, Paul begins his letter with thanksgiving to God for their faith in Christ, their love for each other and their hope of heaven (Colossians 1:4–5). He also promised to pray for them that they would be filled with the knowledge of God's will and grow in all spiritual wisdom and understanding. He followed this with a very moving exposition of the supremacy of Christ over all things (1:15–20). He then addressed the issue of division in the church with both courage and tact, a model for every pastor facing similar difficulties. He did not attack the dissident group directly, but gently warned the believers not to fall into the same errors. In fact, we know only by reading between the lines what the error or, as some would call it, heresy, actually was. He is very positive without being unnecessarily confrontational. Therefore, it is not surprising that scholars disagree on the nature of the problem. It is likely that some of the church members were converts from Judaism, as there were colonies of Jews scattered through the region. Few would have direct contact with Jerusalem. As merchants, they kept to their own community. It is more likely that the Jewish converts were liberal Jews practising a folk religious form of Jewish faith.

The majority of converts would have been local Phrygian people steeped in the folk religion of the Lycus Valley. Since Colossae has never been excavated, we have no detailed knowledge of their religious beliefs, but we know a good deal about the religious life of the region and it is unlikely that Colossae would have been different. My research into both the text and its context has led me to accept the thesis of Clinton Arnold, that the false teaching summarised in Colossians 2:8–23 was an attempt to contextualise the gospel in terms of the worldview, beliefs and practices of the folk religions of the Phrygian regions. The result was a false syncretism of joining together what was incompatible and thereby blurring the uniqueness and finality of Jesus Christ as Saviour and Lord of all creation. The future of the church living in a hostile environment was at stake.

Taking this threat seriously, Paul wrote what I believe to be one of his most important letters for the churches in our modern world. He begins by warning the church not to be taken captive through philosophy and empty deceit (2:8). The verb *sulagogeo* means 'to enslave' or 'kidnap' – an image well understood in the Pacific Islands concerning the slave traders of 150 years ago. Paul has already reminded his readers that they had been rescued from the kingdom of darkness and had received redemption and forgiveness of sins (1:13–14). They are in danger of returning to the same bondage of human wisdom, tradition and worthless deceit (a harsh word!). It seems that some in the church were trying to contextualise their new faith in the context of the religions they had left behind.

I suggest that the reason they were doing this is that they were facing an identity crisis. They were rejoicing in their new identity in Christ, but were confused over their cultural identity. The church was too young to have developed a new theistic cultural identity. In this crisis of cultural identity, the more nationalistic members of the church were attempting to interpret their new faith within the worldview of their previous faith with its rituals, myths and symbols. However, their attempt to contextualise their faith had gone wrong. Although they continued to believe in Jesus Christ and salvation in his name, they had lost the power or *mana* they had found in Christ. They had, perhaps without realising it, shifted their focus from the supremacy of Christ to a trust in the spirit world with which they were so familiar. They had returned to their biocosmic faith.

Paul saw that the very existence of the church was being threatened. He acted promptly by sending this letter, since as a prisoner he was unable to visit them himself. He now intended to do so when he was released from prison and he instructed Philemon to prepare a guestroom for him (Philemon 22). Many of the following elements in their earlier folk religion would be familiar to the people of Melanesia. The people of the Lycus Valley were conscious of their dependence on the world of spirits that surrounded them. Paul called these spirits *stoicheia tou kosmou*, but this is translated as 'elemental spirits of the universe' (NRSV). The inhabitants venerated the friendly spirits as protectors against the hostile demonic spirits that plagued their daily lives. These spirits were also described as 'angelic' (2:18), whom they worshipped or venerated as protectors from sickness, disease and death, as well as from floods, drought and earthquakes, which were frequent in this region.

Some of these spirits were thought of as gods and goddesses, as in the classical Greek world, whose culture had been part of their own. The worship of Artemis, the mother goddess of Asia Minor, the symbol of fertility, was typified by her many breasts; she was the supreme goddess of the Ephesians, as Paul and his companions discovered to their cost (Acts 19:23 41). Throughout the Lycus Valley, Hekale, the goddess of the underworld, was worshipped and feared. She was able to cause sickness and death; as in Melanesia, the cause of sickness and death was not 'how', but 'who caused it?' We know that the valley was full of temples of the gods and goddesses they worshipped. Through the rituals of witchcraft and magic, the worshipper sought to communicate with the living dead. Armlets, charms and spells were used to appease the evil spirits.

Against this background Paul urges the believers not to be enticed back to observing their pagan festivals, including new moon festivals and Sabbaths (the impact of Judaism on pagan religion, 2:16). For these, he said, 'are only a shadow of what is to come, but the substance (or reality) belongs to Christ' (2:17). As shadows have no life of their own, these traditional rituals have no value unless they are seen as means to glorify Christ. In the same way, ascetic practices for the purpose of seeing visions and acts of self-denial have no value in themselves. To boast of one's humility is 'to be puffed up without cause' (2:15).

Paul responds to these misguided practices

First, Paul identifies with the church at Colossae for he understands their struggle with the reality of the spirit world. He was very conscious of the reality of the unseen world, a world of principalities and powers belonging to the dominion of darkness (1:13,16). He was to write to the church in Ephesus that their struggle was not with their flesh and blood but 'against the cosmic powers of this present darkness, against the spiritual forces of evil in the heavenly places' (the non-empirical world, Ephesians 5:12). Many Western theologians don't understand this reality, but Paul did. He was aware of Christ's ministry of casting out evil spirits.

Second, Paul understood that the Christians were struggling with the consequences of their new identity in Christ and their rejection of their culture. He, a Jew called to be an apostle to the gentiles, had gone through the struggles of whether or not to circumcise believers and of eating meat sacrificed to idols. While identifying with the motives of the Colossians, Paul firmly warned them that if contextualising their faith in the rituals of their former religion weakened their trust in Christ and his saving work on the cross, then this was wrong and they must stop returning to these practices. Although Paul does not state categorically the details of these errors, the text suggests that my reconstruct is accurate. It is called syncretism, the joining together of what is irreconcilable. By so doing, they had become guilty of idolatry.

Third, Paul's response was to call the church to confess Jesus Christ as Lord and Saviour over all things including creation, the unseen spirit world, and the church. In Christ, God has reconciled everything to himself; Christ is the visible image of the invisible God (1:15–20). If Christ is truly supreme then there is no place for any other powers. Syncretism would then fail to be an issue.

Fourth, Paul insists that if Christ is Lord then his followers must live lives worthy of him and in a spirit of thankfulness. To be 'in Christ' is to participate in his death to sin and his resurrection to life eternal. The believers must set their minds and hearts on the things of Christ. To do this, they must put to death every personal evil desire and all social behaviour that is immoral (3:5–9). They are to put on the new clothes of compassionate and righteous living (3:10–17). In Christ's church there can be no dichotomy between being and doing, between belief and practice, or between word and deed. Only then will the peace of Christ reign in our hearts. Therefore Christians are to test their ritualistic practices against Christ's ethical standards of personal and social behaviour.

Last, contextualisation was not a private matter. For Paul it involves the whole family – husbands, wives, children and household servants or slaves, living godly lives in harmonious relationships (3:8–4:1). The unit of the church was the family. When I was a pastor in India, I was often asked the size of my congregation. I always replied in terms of the number of families, not the number of communicant members.

Discerning boundaries between contextualisation and syncretism in Melanesia today

I am conscious of one fact. Only the members of the indigenous church can discern the boundaries between contextualisation and syncretism, as together they seek the Lord's will. In his letter Paul outlines principles that must guide their decisions. The church must decide how to implement them. Likewise today no missionary or person of one culture can make these decisions for people of another culture. The early missionaries in Melanesia did not always recognise this. Christ bequeathed to the church his Holy Spirit with the promise that 'when he, the Spirit of truth comes, he will guide you with all the truth' (John 16:13).

In the light of Paul's response to the divisive issues (or heresies) in the Colossian church, I offer the following principles as guidelines to help Melanesian church members discern the boundaries between good contextualisation and bad syncretism.

1. Contextualisation is essential to the Church in mission

The gospel is good news for everyone, irrespective of their cultural heritage. The church's missiological task is to know Christ and to make him known to all peoples, each in their own cultural context. The Lord from Heaven who became Jesus of Nazareth is our supreme model of contextualisation. If Paul and Peter had failed to contextualise the gospel for the gentiles, as Paul did in Athens and Peter at Joppa, then Christianity would have remained a Jewish sect and eventually died. Contextualisation calls for great courage and patience in understanding both the message and cultural contexts of Scripture and the religion and culture of the recipient people. The gospel has first to judge us in our culture before we can share it with others in their cultures. In humility, we must take care that our own prejudices do not blind others to God's word. We all wear culturally tinted glasses.

2. The dangers of syncretism

If interpreting the content of the gospel in the cultural forms of the worldview and religious practices of our traditional religions and cultures weakens Christ's Lordship over our lives or blurs our understanding of salvation through the Cross, then the process has become syncretistic and must be rejected. This is what was happening in Colossae. In order to identify with the people of the land and their former culture, some of the Colossians were interpreting the gospel in the worldview of their former folk religion and culture so that Christ alone was no longer supreme in their lives. The unity and future of the church at Colossae was at stake. It was in danger of being absorbed back into its pagan past.

3. Traditional rituals, myths and symbols need to be transformed if they are to be effective vehicles of the church's mission

Traditional practices are useful bridges in sharing Christ's love and righteousness, but only when they point to Christ and his kingdom. They are not an end in themselves. For example, the coastal fish festival of singing and dancing, which may last for several months, is an integral part of Papua New Guinean culture. It is a festival central to the people's identity and human dignity. It brings together the religious, social, artistic, economic and health concerns of the people. Some aspects of the festival are open to demonic spirit control and must be rejected. However, the joy and universal truths in the festival can be redeemed and used to strengthen faith in Christ.

Overseas missionaries are ill-equipped to judge this matter. The local and national church, through prayer and consultation, must discern God's will for themselves. Don McGregor's monograph, *The Fish and the Cross* (privately published), offers a helpful discussion on the often divisive festival. The pig festival of inland villages is another festival in need of transformation. Every cultic practice, whether Christian or otherwise, is in need of constant purification, renewal and transformation into the image of Christ.

4. Do not let your practice be a stumbling block to others

If participating in any traditional religious or cultural belief or practice becomes a stumbling block in the church, and causes some of its members to fall away in unbelief or unrighteousness, or to divide the church, then the church should refrain from participating in such practices. Then it is better not to adopt such practices in the church's worship or mission outreach. Paul addressed this problem over food sacrificed to idols in the pagan temples and then sold in the marketplace. He urged the church at Corinth to be careful about those whose weak conscience might be wounded by their eating such meat (1 Corinthians 8:1–13). The church can move forward only when the congregation is of one mind.

5. In controversial issues much patience, prayer and mutual love is needed

If the focus of the church is to build up faith in Christ, godly living and commitment to Christ's mission in the world, then controversial cultural practices in the liturgy and witness must not be allowed to become central. They must be kept peripheral to the church's life or rejected altogether. At the present, one such issue that is dividing the Western Church is the ordaining of practicing homosexuals. Truth and love must go together in discerning God's will. Any attempt to manipulate people's opinions or votes must be resisted. Righteousness and love for another must prevail. The issue of slavery is a classic example. Paul returned Onesimus, the runaway slave, now converted, to his master Philemon with a letter asking Philemon to treat him as a dear brother in Christ (Philemon 15–16). In the Roman Empire, the church was a catalyst for the freeing of slaves. But it took time. Much patience, prayer and a spirit of forgiveness was needed then and is still needed. Today, in our rapidly changing cultures, patience and love must prevail.

The Entry of Christianity onto Mota Island, 1857–1910

Cea Brian

Introduction: Christianity's entry onto Mota

The arrival of Christianity onto the island of Mota is an interesting story because many of the Anglican Christian ceremonies first took place here. The island of Mota is one of smallest islands in the Banks group. According to history, it was separated from the island of Vanua-lava, forming a separate land with many rocks. Two groups of people who first lived there formed the two family lines which are there today. The language they first used was Qet language (Qet is the name of a god from the Banks people); it was used in the Mission work in teaching, translation etc., and is still used today.

People who first lived on this island before Christianity arrived were totally dominated by secret societies and were deeply influenced by witchcraft. They didn't know that there were other people different from them, namely, white people. In the year 1857, they saw white men for the first time. They thought these people were the spirits of their ancestors who had died long ago and had come back to visit them. In fact, these white people were the missionaries, Bishop George Augustus Selwyn and his colleagues. Later the local natives understood that these white people were real people with different colour skin and coming from a different country. They had come to do something for them that was good. They understood later that they had come to bring them Christianity, the good news of Jesus Christ.

After the arrival of this group of people, there came black-birders and then the British and French Governments; their arrival also affected a lot of people on the island. However, it was missionaries who arrived first on the island. The missionaries collected boys to go to New Zealand, converted them to Christianity, trained them for mission and then returned them to the island to evangelise their own people. The island's outstanding person in this era of local ministry was George Sarawia who was ordained as the first Priest of Melanesia in the year 1873 and then did most of the work of evangelisation on the island. After him, others worked as missionaries on the other islands of Vanuatu as well as in other Melanesian Countries, sharing the Good News of Jesus Christ.

Part 1: The island of Mota

Geographical location

The islands of the Pacific Ocean have had the reputation of being an untouched paradise. Vanuatu, in the South West Pacific, is the country where Mota is situated. Mota is one of the islands forming the Torba Province. It is a small island situated in the north of Vanuatu and is located in the North East of Torba Province. In shape, it is almost circular with a high hill in the centre perhaps 200 feet tall, with a plain surrounding it, forming a hat shape from side view.

It is about two hours walk around the island so it is about nine to ten kilometres in circumference. The coastlines of the island are rough and steep, and there are no harbours good enough for ships or boats to hide in bad weather. Mota is best known in Anglican history as one of the first Melanesian Christian islands.[60]

Background information

In the past there lived two people, one named Nolmemea from Vanua-lava living close to where Torba Provincial Government is now located, and another was Peitanasqe from Mota-lava. These two men were made friends through *Sukwe* (a pre-Christian Ceremonial society of rank with the traditional amassing of wealth and prestige by spells). They performed the ceremony at Mota-lava, helping each other. This ceremony enabled them to travel from one to the other of these two islands. Peitanasqe looked South and saw a tiny hill sticking out from the sea. He asked his friend Nolememea what it was that was sticking out from the sea like an island. His friend looked at it closely and agreed that it was really an island. They stood and wondered how that land was formed for it was the first time they saw it.

Suddenly Nolememea looked down onto Vanua-lava and saw a big chasm there, because part of the island had disappeared. So he told Peitanasqe that the small island had come out from Vanua-lava. They called this small island 'Motarig', meaning 'small bushes on top of the hill'. If ever you travel to Vanua-lava where Torba Province is located, you will notice a big harbour; it was believed that at one time there was land where the harbour is, but this land had moved out to form the small island of Mota. This island, when it was still part of Vanua-lava, was the most comfortable part of Vanua-lava; stones were erected there for the god Qet to have a rest. That is why there are so many stones today at the top of Mota island.

When Peitanasqe and Nolememea first discovered the island, they made plans to find someone who would be first to live there. Nolememea was to look for someone at Vanua-lava and Peitanasqe at Mota-lava. Nolememea found two women at Vanua-lava, one was

Rofte (with her two sons, Tekula and Manmaneula), and another was Wokar. These two women were sisters who came from Saqon (the area where Nolememea came from) and were the first people to live on Mota.[61]

Language

When these two women and their children first came to live on Mota, they brought with them the Qet language that was said to be a very respectful language and of great value. It was because of this that Christian missionaries adopted it to use for the mission of the church in Melanesia. There were two languages at Mota when missionaries first arrived, different only in sounds or times of speaking. This second language was believed to be the language of those who came later, and named after the family from Saqon.

When the Qet language was adopted by the mission, then the other language disappeared, so the Qet (or Mota) language spread all over the Banks islands, to other islands in Vanuatu, and even to the Solomons. This language was chosen for the reason that no Melanesian language is richer and more suitable or easier for Europeans to learn. When this language was used, it spread through the Melanesian teachers to more than 10,000 Melanesians by the late 1800's, and the translation of the Bible into other languages was generally made from the Mota version. This language was used in teaching and learning until 1930 when a general staff conference of mission schools decided that English should be the language of teaching in the missions' boarding schools.[62]

People

In one of the Qet history stories, two small groups of people were building their *nakamal* when heavy rain stopped them, spreading them into two groups, one on one side of the house and the other group on the other side, with the roof separating them. The god Qet had been thinking how he could separate the few people into two family lines, so the separation in the house gave him a chance, and he divided the people into two family lines according to where they stood on each side of the house. People on one side of the house were permitted to find their partners with those on the other side of the house, but not from among themselves.

Today people still follow these two family lines called Saqon and Tatalai. Saqon means darkness or night and derives from the story of how Qet created all things. He created everything but he did not create darkness for the people to rest. He was asked at Vanua-lava for darkness, so he went to the Torres Islands to bring darkness to Vanua-lava. The place at Vanua-lava where he landed was then called Saqon, meaning 'night', for Qet bought darkness there. It was people from there who first went to live on Mota. Tatalai means 'denying their homeland'. When people from Saqon saw those who came later, they denied them. That is why the name Tatalai was given to the other family line.

These two groups of people first lived on Mota and formed the two family lines. The people multiplied until there were many people living all around the island. When missionaries first arrived on Mota, they found that the total population of people at the time was about two thousand. Mota had that population when it was fully evangelised but because of sickness and black magic coming over from Queensland, and the kidnapping of Mota people by whites, the number began to reduce very quickly.[63]

Cultural aspect

Missionaries arrived when people were living in eighteen villages namely Losara, Maua, Qarangwis, Anuarara, Louta, Salte, Sareara-ara, Takeluarea, Lovatnigin, Nomatrin, Pakasaroa, Ratona, Salaima, Taligtamur, Paramata, Malcansa, Asuetag and Lenamara.

People of those days were not allowed to go to other villages for they were continually at war, dominated by secret societies, steeped in witchcraft, given to kava drinking and without real chiefs. The only special time they met was in the secret society called Sukwe. Many ceremonies were made and one was a Kolekole. In a Kolekole people who belong to this secret society were to pull a house to pieces to compel the owner to offer his son to join them.

It was said that people of the past were very big people; honour and respect for their chiefs and for each individual was very important. Chiefs and highly respected people in those days were those who ate the 'um' (taboo fire). Those who completed twelve Ums took the rank of a 'Tavusmelle' (highest chiefly rank), and were more highly respected in the community. It was because of this great respect that Mota easily accepted Christianity, for people respected their chiefs, and it was from the chiefs that missionaries first sought permission to introduce Christianity.[64]

Part 2: Mota exposed to outside influences

The missionaries

Missionaries first came to Melanesia in 1835 when the Methodists sent their missionaries to Fiji. Later the London Missionary Society sent Samoan missionaries to the New Hebrides (Vanuatu) and to the Loyalty islands in 1939. The Presbyterians began work in the New Hebrides in 1848 when John Geddie planted Christianity in Aneityum, an island in the southern part of the country.

These islands were among the most savage and cruel of Melanesia, but in spite of early disasters, the Presbyterian

Missionaries pressed on so hard that they won over the chief of Aneityum. The Roman Catholic Mission went to the Solomons in 1845 with Jean Baptist Epalle as the leader and he became the first bishop of Melanesia and Micronesia.

The Anglican mission in Melanesia was founded by Bishop Selwyn in 1849 when he visited New Caledonia and the Loyalty islands taking five young Melanesians to be educated in New Zealand. He came to the Southern New Hebrides in that same year (1849) and later went further north to the Banks islands. Thus missionaries were the first people to show their presence to the natives of Mota as people different from themselves. They were the first white men for Mota people to see; for the Mota people these missionaries seemed so strange at first.

The first missionary to arrive on Mota was the Anglican Missionary Bishop, George Augustus Selwyn with his men, in the year 1857. He had made his first voyage through Melanesia in 1848 and found that there were a great number of heathen islands. This moved him to evangelise them. His view for this work was to bring some young people to Auckland, train them there for Christian Mission and send them back to their home islands to do the work.

In 1849, he made his first recruiting voyage to Melanesia and took five boys from the Loyalty Islands. He did not take one from the New Hebrides although he reached the southern islands. He made voyages for the same purpose the following years and may have taken some boys from the southern New Hebrides. In 1857 he made another recruiting voyage to Melanesia and went further north to the Banks islands. The ship went ashore at Vanua-lava, and then to Mota where the natives ventured out to the ship in swarms, in little bits of canoes roughly made; they climbed up the deck and jumped down again, making fun. John Palmer, an Australian Missionary Priest to Melanesia who was with the bishop at that time says 'our decks were crowded with native brown bodies who made an endless din'. The scene was very beautiful, such rich colours, unimaginable shades of green, along the shore were brown bodies, a bright chocolate in contrast with the dark green foliage.

He also recorded how strange it was to be surrounded by a heap of native brown bodies. The natives at first thought that missionaries were the spirits of those who had died long before and had come back to visit them, so they were very frightened; but later came a change of feeling. As the missionaries entered the villages, their arrival caused great excitement, the children jumping up and down, clapping their hands and shouting, and the whole population coming out of their houses and surrounding them. The natives were very glad as they saw the white men and welcomed them happily in their villages.

The history on Mota was not like the history on other islands where missionaries really suffered in order to calm the people and to teach them. In many other places, ships were not allowed to anchor or go ashore. The main reason why Mota was not like that was that traders and black birders had not yet arrived there to steal from the people. Missionaries continued to visit the island until natives knew well who those people were and what they had come to do.[65]

Blackbirders, traders and colonial influence

History states that explorers were the first people to sail to Vanuatu waters. In the order of the time of their arrival, De Quiros Spanish came first, in the year 1606; James Cook a British explorer came in 1774; Bouganville, French in 1778, and William Blight, British in 1789. These people came in their boats exploring the lands, passing close to our islands but with no chance to go ashore onto many islands in Vanuatu. Blackbirders were to come soon afterwards; later came Missionaries and other traders and then the Colonial influence of the British and French.

In Mota the blackbirders' group of people came in some considerable time after the arrival of missionaries. I believe it happened this way because so many of the bigger islands in the southern part of the country stopped the blackbirders from going further north. Another view is that it has been God's way to work like that. For as God chose Israel, a small nation, in revealing His ways, so he chose Mota a small island to be the best known and remembered in the church of Melanesia (Anglican Church). It was in Mota that many Christian ceremonies were first performed or celebrated (see Part 4, below).

The first stealing of Mota natives was for work in the sugarcane plantations in Queensland and Fiji. Many of the natives were stolen in those years from 1890s onwards. Traders used a lie to collect people. They enticed the Mota people with the promise of collecting for themselves tools that they needed such as pots, knives, axes, clothes, to make life easier for them. Because of this great need, Mota people agreed to go, only to find that they were 'working as if they were labourers'. This continued for many, many years.

Patteson discovered this practice in 1894 when people told him that some men had been taken by a ship that they called a 'thief ship'. When missionaries found this out, they also noted that the depopulation of the island was very rapid during those years, and realised later in the early 1900s that although the old slave trade to Fiji and Queensland was a thing of the past, labour was being recruited excessively for the British and French plantations of the New Hebrides.

There were also many cases of the illegal recruiting of women wanted as companions for the labourers on these plantations, taking even some from their husbands, for under the dual government of the condominium, no woman was safe in her home and no people had rights over their own homes. In the face of this serious injustice, Christianity took its part to fight the evils of those labour traders and commanded all people on the island not to go down to the beach when those ships called again.[66]

Part 3: Introduction of a new religion – Christianity on Mota

Christianity is a worldwide religion founded on Jesus Christ and his earthly ministry, and all who followed Christ's teachings called themselves Christians. Jesus Christ in his earthly ministry first called twelve men to be his followers and at all times they were always with him, until the time he was arrested and killed. After His resurrection, just before he ascended into heaven, he commanded his followers to go into every nation and make people his disciples, baptizing them in the name of the Father and of the Son and of the Holy Spirit (Matthew 28:16–20).

Jesus' disciples did not forget what he commanded; they did what he told them and found that their work was very successful. People responded to what the disciples taught and soon there were many followers preaching the Good News of Jesus Christ. This mission work continued for many hundreds of years so that many nations became influenced by Christianity.

The Christian religion was first introduced and accepted in the New Hebrides (Vanuatu) in the year 1848, when Geddie planted it on Aneityum[67], and on Mota in the year 1857, when it was planted by Bishop George Augustus Selywn.[68] People gladly accepted this religion but it was with fear that it might do away with their cultures. However, Mota people saw Christianity as something so special to them that they showed the white man their support by helping them in all they needed. Soon Mota language was adapted for mission work, the first school was established there (except the one at Lifou which was established just before); many Christian conversions and ceremonies first took place there and it also provided the first Melanesian priest and many teachers to other islands.[69]

The Anglican mission

The Christian church over its history became divided between the East and the West (in the 11th century), and then in the sixteenth century the Reformation in the West led to the establishment of other Christian traditions. The Catholic Church became known as the Roman Catholic Church, while other churches were created during this time, breaking away from Rome over disagreements in the beliefs of the church. The Church of England (the Anglican Church) with King Henry VIII as the Head was one of these new churches. As this church became more mature and equipped, it spread through the missionaries to other countries including into Melanesia.

The most famous figure in the Anglican Mission in Melanesia was Bishop George Augustus Selwyn. In the early 1840s he was made bishop and was in charge of a new diocese consisting of New Zealand and the Southern Melanesian islands from 1846-1848. He was appointed chaplain on the boat 'Dido' on her voyage to Rotuma, New Caledonia and Vanuatu.[70] On Aneityum, he discovered Presbyterian Missionaries who landed there ahead of him, so he and John Geddie established a friendly working relationship with the hope of evangelising the whole of Vanuatu, giving Geddie and the Presbyterians the southern islands and Selwyn and the Anglicans the north.[71] So Selwyn made regular visits to the Melanesian islands. In 1857 when he went to Mota Island with the teachings of Anglicanism.

The province of Melanesia and its background structure

When in 1847 the active churchman Bishop Selwyn made his first visit to the Pacific after his consecration as the first bishop of New Zealand, he was given an order by the Archbishop of Canterbury, to do something for the people of the Pacific. His visits to the Pacific were very important. A ship was funded for the purpose. A young priest John Coleridge Patteson helped him in the work and later continued to be a great leader for the Melanesian mission.[72]

In 1861, Bishop Selwyn formed the Missionary Diocese of Melanesia within the Church of the Province of New Zealand. He and the other bishops of New Zealand consecrated Patteson as the first bishop of that diocese on 24 February 1861. Patteson continued the work of the Melanesian mission that Selwyn had begun.[73]

The diocese of Melanesia continued to grow with more bishops being appointed. The diocese became stronger and stronger, and it came a point when the area was too large and there were too few bishops.[74] Cecil John Wood, the fourth bishop of the diocese of Melanesia, wrote to mission staff that there should be native councils in the Melanesian church to teach the people the habit of thinking and talking over church matters so that some may learn to assume responsibilities. He also stated that the church must be the church of the local country, not of a foreign country. He wanted the future Melanesian Church to be self-governing, self-supporting and self-extending. He had been preparing the ground for this new future but resigned from his position in 1918.[75]

John Manwaring Steward became the fifth bishop of Melanesia (1919–28). In one of his conferences, four questions were raised; one of them was: 'should the diocese be divided?' He had in mind several things which he wished to do – to establish a synod, to increase the number of Melanesian Clergy, to extend the work of Mission to others islands, and to obtain assistant bishops, leading on to division of his diocese and making the way for the establishment of an oceanic province. In a conference at Marovovo, the majority of people opposed the division of the diocese for political and economic reasons.[76] Many of Steward's plans failed. However he had prepared the way for the future. He submitted his plans during the first year of his episcopate and he finally summoned his first synod and staff conference in October 1921 at Siota, for the purpose of governing and regulating the affairs of the diocese. Another synod was held in 1924 where it was decided to ask the General Synod of New Zealand to enact a Canon to the effect that the New Zealand bishops should not elect a bishop of Melanesia without the agreement of the Synod of the Diocese.[77]

In 1920, a conference of Australia and New Zealand bishops had resolved that the time had come for the formation of the New Diocese of Melanesian Mission, New Britain, New Ireland, the Bismarck Archipelago and the Northern Solomons. It was also agreed that the steps that could be taken for the creation of any new diocese should rest with the General Synod of New Zealand, and further steps could be carried through as agreed upon between the General Synods of New Zealand and Australia. In the end, no new diocese was formed, but assistant bishops were elected to help in the work.[78]

After a few years of working and further developments under other bishops, John Wallace of Australia who worked in Papua New Guinea as a priest and as an assistant bishop, was chosen by the synod of Melanesia to be their new bishop and was enthroned in Honiara in 1967. He came with many new ideas. The biggest change he made was to get permission from the Province of New Zealand to create separate diocese in Melanesia. As a result, four separated diocese were formed in Melanesia: Central Melanesia, Isabel, Malaita and New Hebrides (Vanuatu).

Bishop John Chisholm became bishop of Central Melanesia and also Archbishop of Melanesia, Bishop Dudley Tuti of Isabel, Bishop Lenard Algfuki of Malaita, and Bishop Rawcliff of the New Hebrides (Vanuatu). The Archbishop of New Zealand and other Church leaders from overseas came and the service of the Inauguration of the Province of Melanesia took place in St. Barnabas Cathedral in Honiara on 26 January 1975.[79] The Church of the Province of Melanesia covers two countries, namely Solomon Islands and the Republic of Vanuatu and also extends to New Caledonia. The church is organised and structured as in the illustration on the following page.[80]

[Insert Diagram]

Approach of the evangelists

Bishops Selwyn and Patteson called at Vanua Lava on the first ship, the 'Southern Cross' in 1857 for the purpose of collecting young boys to study in New Zealand and returning to evangelise their own lands. The first approach they made was to get to know the names of the islands and important leaders whom they could talk to in order to start their work. Natives went down to the beach to see what they'd never seen before. They were asked through sign language for the words for 'you', 'he', 'me', 'I', 'two', 'all of us', etc. These were all written down in the Mota Language. People looked very surprised as missionaries understood Mota language so quickly and could speak it properly.[81] In those days there were still great numbers of people and they all gathered together to see the bishop and his men. People treated the bishop just like one of their own people for he made friends with them through showing kindness, sitting together in meeting places, and exchanging goods with them such as tools and food. People saw these white people as good friends because of their understanding approach.

Another reason for the good relationship between the missionaries and the local people was that the natives already had the practice of showing respect to their leaders. Because of this, they showed respect also to the missionaries, and so Christianity was easily accepted. After making friends with the people, they persuaded a young boy named Sarawia to go on board with them. However, Sarawia refused for he was not sure whether these strangers were really good friends or were planning to kill him. The missionaries then left and promised to be back after eight months.[82]

The following year, the bishop arrived and as he saw Sarawia; he called him by name and told him that if he had followed them to New Zealand, he would have returned home again by now. Sarawia came to believe that these men were really good people for they returned at the very time they had promised. At that visit Sarawia was again invited and at last he agreed to go, for they told him it was a good time for him to go with them. He saw it as a chance to collect for himself tools such as knives, axes, pots, and hammers which he thought could be collected[83]. Another of his thoughts was to see where the white men's country was and how they lived. He did not understand that the bishop wished to teach him another view of life, one which would not decay as material things do. So in the end, Sarawia sailed away with the bishop to New Zealand where he was taught the Good News, was baptised in 1863 and confirmed in 1865. In 1867 he returned to Mota where he set up a model School and Christian villages, with the help of Patteson and his friends who had been some months on the island when Sarawia was away on his study. These men included Pritt, John Palmer and some Norfolkers.[84]

Part 4: Formation of a local church

The first Christian conversions

When Sarawia and other boys were taken to New Zealand, Bishop Patteson and his men did not leave the island on its own but continued to visit the people, learning their language and teaching them the Christian faith. Sarawia was the first Mota converted in New Zealand.

The first baptism on Mota took place at Namatiu village. The year was unknown as it happened in a way that when missionaries came onto the island, they set their headquarters at Lomake where they built their houses and a church. At Lomake, during one of Patteson's visits, he preached an evangelistic sermon, calling for repentance, and it was very challenging. A man who came from Namatiu was touched by the message. He had in his home a son who was very ill. After the sermon, he asked Patteson what to do about his son, so Patteson went and baptised him. This is recorded as the first baptism on the island.[85]

The second baptism was that of a chief of Lomake named Taqale. He was a big chief and the only remaining cannibal on the island. Patteson approached him first for he knew that if he could convince Taqale to accept Christianity, he would give permission for all at Lomake to be baptised. Taqale became a Christian and was baptised. Sarawia returned home and everyone on the island came to be converted, baptised, confirmed and the first eucharist was celebrated.

Patteson set up catechist schools where people from other Banks Islands came to learn from him and from the others who had trained in New Zealand. Church houses were built in other villages and run by local catechists. Many local leaders came from the island and later travelled to other islands to do the mission work because they felt that there was something so good in their lives that should also be given to others. From baptism came confirmations and later two couples asked for Christian marriages. All these took place at Lomake and are stated in the Melanesian history of the Anglican Church as the first Christian ceremonies taking place in Mota.[86]

Local leadership

Christianity first took root in Mota and from there was spread to other islands by leaders who were mostly local teachers. Many Mota people trained in New Zealand and later went to other countries and other islands for the work of evangelism. They included George

Sarawia, Edward Wogale, Robert Pantutun and Maros Tamata. Sarawia did most of the work on the island of Mota until he died in 1901. His last words for the encouragement of people to live a faithful Christian life were 'All is finished; l am setting out on a voyage with a fair wind. O that I shall not turn back but keep on a straight course. There remain the good life and peace; I am not taking that away, follow that.'[87]

Edward Wogale was one of Patteson's pupils who went to Kohimarama in 1863. After his studies there, he was sent to Gela (in the Solomons) as a missionary. In 1876, he worked as a missionary in Fiji and with the Solomon Island Kanakas. Later in that same year he went to Torres as their first missionary and established the church there. In 1880, he made another visit to Gela and then returned to Torres where he died in the year 1883. He was seen as the most intelligent of the Melanesian Priests, establishing a close friendship with Patteson.[88]

Robert Pantutun was another student of Patteson ordained in the year 1872 and was sent as a missionary to Santa Maria (Gaua) and then to Maewo and Torres after Wogale's death. After his works there, he returned to Mota in the year 1910 and died there.[89]

Maros Tamata was also a Mota Missionary. He was one of Mota's brilliant men who was like a son to John Palmer. He started a small school in Logona (Gaua) in the year 1878 and taught there for seven years.[90] He was ordained in the year 1884 and was one of the best of the Melanesian Priests. He did excellent work at Logona, baptising fifty-three people on that part of the island.

Another of Mota's local leaders in the church was Ulgau who was sent to Raga as a missionary. He had been persuaded at Norfolk by his friend Louis Tariliu from Raga who had seen that it was hard to do the work alone in his own home. It was those two that brought the Good News to Raga. They started the first school there, but it was not them alone; Ulgau brought with him a Mota man named Maslea who helped to evangelise part of Raga. Ulgau died in Raga in the year 1904. He was seen as one of the best and humblest of all Melanesian teachers. Bishops Selwyn and Wilson tried to ordain him but he said he was not worthy of that position and the only thing he wanted was to evangelise the heathen.[91] He worked six years there and twenty-three Christians were baptised at Bwatvenue – the only Christians on Raga. There were many more Mota teachers after those notable people had gone out with the Good News of Christ.

Conclusion

Today we ni-Vanuatu are proud to say that our country is a Christian country. Everyone who says this should always remember the good work of the early missionaries, for it was through them that we have received Christianity. From the history of our islands we understand that missionaries who came in to our islands really suffered hardships. We know what the situation was like. Indigenous people were totally influenced by their cultural traditions in their societies and never knew God or people different from themselves. They only came to realise this as missionaries first approached them.

The missionaries had to learn their language, traditions and behaviour, and began their teachings as if they were clearing dark bushes where much dirt had to be thrown away; and they planted new seeds, for many practices in the cultures had to be discarded and replaced with the new teachings. In Mota, as well as in the whole Church of Melanesia, people still remember the work of Bishop Selwyn, Bishop Patteson and George Sarawia, and the others who brought the Good News into other islands, through the eucharist and a special thanksgiving feast which is made every year. I am glad to say that Mota is developing economically and spiritually in the life of the church as the result of the work of the early missionaries.

Leaders in the church should remember that although we say Vanuatu is a Christian country, there are still heathen people in parts of some of our islands. It is the duty of Christians to convert them. Special thanks should be given to the Melanesian brotherhood and other mission workers in other denominations who are carrying out this work in order to bring them into God' family.

Finally, I would like to thank God for the courage, willingness, faith and love he gave our missionaries like Selwyn and Patteson to bring the Good News into our islands. May God's grace continue to rest with them in paradise.

Bibliography

Fox, E. C., *Lord of the Southern Isles: Being the Story of the Anglican Mission in Melanesia 1849-1949*, London: A. R. Mowbray & Co., Limited, 1958

Miller, J. G. *Live Book 1: A History of Church Planting in the New Hebrides to 1880*, Sydney: Presbyterian Church of Australia, 1978

Miller, J. G. *Live Book 3: A History of Church Planting in Vanuatu to 1880*, Port Vila: Presbyterian Church of Vanuatu, 1985

Interviews

Fr. Ezekiel Tias
Mr. Fred Sagler
Fr. John Bennett
Mr. Lancilot Wollemaro
Mr. Stanley Womack

Part Three

Other Contemporary Issues

Tension within the Evangelical Protestant Church of Vanuatu

Lionel Tom

Introduction

There are so many problems in the churches of the world today. Satan uses many of his techniques to try to pull down the church, of which Christ is the head. Today when there is a problem, the whole church is paralysed. It does not function correctly, just as a motor vehicle cannot function properly when something goes wrong. We need to find out what the problem is and fix it. This is the same in the life of the church; we need to know what has caused the problem that is preventing it from functioning properly, and fix it.

Therefore in this paper I shall look at the problems that have caused the Evangelical Protestant Church of Vanuatu (*Eglise Evangelique*) not to function as it should. I will not only look at the problems, but also try to find out the causes of them and suggest how we can solve them. I will point to some suggestions and examples of the organisation of the church found in the Bible that I consider helpful for the running of any church that faces similar problems.

History of the Protestant Church – Settlement of the first missionary, the first convert and the first church planted

Before the Protestant Church (that is, the Free Evangelical Church) came to Vanuatu, there was a man called Monsieur Bergeret from Noumea, New Caledonia, who was the first person to seek a more active co-operation between the church in New Caledonia and the Presbyterian Church in the New Hebrides (PCNH). At the General Assembly of the Presbyterian Church in 1939, Doctor Frater of the New Hebrides Presbyterian Mission was asked to look into this request and make further contact. Unfortunately, this did not take place as World War II was declared, closing all doors for further contact at that point. The hope was nearly gone until there was a chance meeting when a man called Graham Miller from the PCNH and his family stopped off in Noumea in 1943 (on their way back to New Zealand). He was able to talk with Pastor Rene Brabant and raise the issue once again.

Following this discussion, Pastor Brabant was able to do some research and raise the issue at the next General Assembly of the PCNH, which he attended on the island of Tangoa (off the mainland of Espiritu Santo) in 1948. At the General Assembly, the Rev. Murray of Nguna was appointed to initiate the concept of the two churches working together. In 1951, Rev. Marc Lacheret from New Caledonia attended the General Assembly of PCNH held at Nguna. At this meeting he addressed the members about the need for a Protestant mission, as at that time there were ni-Vanuatu people working in Noumea and there were students there who needed a pastor's care. At the same time he asked if his church could send New Caledonian pastors to serve alongside the pastors of the Presbyterian Church of the New Hebrides. His request was accepted and at that time the two churches agreed to work together.

The General Assembly allocated the following areas as mission fields for the Protestant Church of New Caledonia: Hog Harbour (on the island Espiritu Santo), Malo (an island off Espiritu Santo), and the Malekulan colony of heathen people in North Malekula. Following the invitation of the Presbyterian Church, the Protestant Mission of New Caledonia depended on the Mission Society of Paris to send the first missionaries to the New Hebrides in 1952. These first missionaries were Pastor Billy Magulue and a teacher named Kare Siorem.

Pastor Billy Magulue and his legacy

Pastor Billy was based on Wala Island on Malekula, a Presbyterian village, and he started to evangelise the people known as the Big Nambas and the Small Nambas. These people were still heathen and not reached by the gospel. The two groups were fighting over some pigs that had been killed and over a woman who had become the wife of a chief. At that time the Big Nambas' chief (Kali) had 22 wives and the Small Nambas' chief (Matan) had 3 wives.

In 1952, Pastor Katawa Watu and a builder, Jean Kafeat, came and joined Pastor Billy on Malekula. Pastor Katawa and his family were based at the village of Orap. The first heathen people to come and stay were from the Small Nambas tribe. They stayed together with an old man called Tebit who was the landowner at that time. This man was very friendly with the Presbyterians. This community of Small Nambas later became the centre of the young church and the centre of the FELP (French Education Federation Protestant).

In 1953, Pastor Katawa moved to Hog Harbour, Santo, to serve there. Jean Kafeat remained on Wala with his wife and it was he who built the school with the help of the local people using local timber and materials. The school was completed in 1953. The first teachers were Pastor Ita and Pastor Drill Treulu, who were based at Pinalun, a Presbyterian village where a temporary school had been built. The creation of the school was possible due to the kindness of a chief called Jack. This chief was also a Presbyterian and close friend of Pastor Drill. In the following year, 1954, a village of heathen people left the bush and came to settle at a place called Bethel. Those who came were from the Small Nambas. They were able to start a village near the sea through the kindness of a Presbyterian elder who had given them the land. The Pinalun School was transferred to this place in 1955. A teacher called Tidjine Joseph Niane and his family came to join Pastor Drill and help in the work at this village.

In 1956, Ajapunya Pamani and his family came to take the place of Joseph who was teaching at Bethel. Joseph moved to Orap that same year. Pastor Billy had a ship called *Rachel*, which helped take people to the Norsup Hospital. This ship was also used to transport teachers and missionaries, and it was used to transport goods from the Ballande store in Santo to Malekula. The ship *Rachel* had been bought from a missionary of the Presbyterian Church based at Aulua, East Malekula.

In 1957, Ajapunya Tamumu came to stay at Ipayato as a nurse. There was, however, a problem with housing and so he was moved to Malekula and settled on the island of Atchin, were he started a school. During the same year a school was opened in the village of Rembeck.

The Big Nambas first came to settle at a place called Tevit. This land was given to them by an old man who was himself a former Big Nambas. Pastor Ita was the first man to work in this village as pastor and teacher at the same time.

In 1958 and 1959, Ajapunya Tamumu and some teachers started to reach out to the Small Nambas. At that time Nathan was their chief. This was a continuation of the work of Pastor Billy who had left in 1958. Ajapunya was acting as a nurse in the beginning as he was not yet a pastor. Later in 1959 they started to preach the gospel to the Small Nambas. In previous times Pastor Drill would go on outreach journeys with an Australian missionary of the Presbyterian Church named Alex Peerman. The last of the Small Nambas who converted (including chief Natan) came and settled in Netune later in 1960. In 1962 another school was opened in Benavet and Nanyakarawa. Moses was the first teacher, and was followed by teacher Masrvoas. In 1972 the school at the village of Wiawi was opened.

Kare Siorem and his legacy

Kare Siorem was based at Saramy, Santo, with a plantation owner called Master My, a French Protestant who decided to start a school for the children of his workers. Kilak Newman became the first teacher of the FELP. He had gone to Santo because there was no school in Malekula as yet. When Kare went to the bush he not only visited the heathen people, but also made maps of the area that was already evangelised and that which was not.

On one of his longer trips, which took about a month, Kare took with him an anthropologist, Jean Guillard, and acted as his guide. This same man, Guillard, organised a trip to New Caledonia for the big chief of South Santo, Molivalivo. This chief was well known for his power and popularity. It was this chief who ruled over the heathen tribes on the south side of Santo. He lived in the old custom ways and yet was a member of the consulting council of Port Vila – an important body at that time of the nation's history. On one of chief Molivalivo's visits to New Caledonia he asked Raymon Charlemagne to send someone to his village as a nurse in New Hebrides. At that time Billy Magulue was in charge of the mission. The chief was not at all interested in education or religion, but health was a major concern at that point in history. Ajapunya was sent there but, as stated before, he could not stay due to a lack of housing provided for him.

In 1957, Charlemagne was suspended from the main Protestant church. He decided to form a new branch of Free Protestants and many villages joined him in this new break-away. In 1958, Kare Siorem opened up a school among the tribe at Ipayato, but soon had to return home due to the bad mental state of his wife. In June of that same year Chief Molivalivo died. The death of the big chief discouraged many, for the nurse that he had promised had not come. A lot of the bush people then returned to where they had came from.

An arrangement had been made by the administrator Lamadiere and Charlemagne for a nurse to be sent to Ipayato. Finally in April 1960, Ajapunya returned to Ipayato. Before going to Ipayato, Lamadiere instructed the nurse that he should not preach the gospel. The people were not interested in the gospel so Tamumu visited the villagers and encouraged them to come down near the sea and settle there so he could treat them better. As result of this visit the number of the students in the new school at Ipayato grew from seventeen to fifty. Tamumu then asked for New Caledonia to send another teacher. Tamumu held private worship services in his home with the teachers Tidjine and Podia. The people were not interested at all. However, Chief John came and saw Tamumu and said, 'I know that the God of Caledonia is the true God of love and for this reason you have a great love for us. Now I take this God for me and my people also.'

This great event in the history of the church, when Chief John received the gospel with his people, was in July 1960. Chief John with Tamumu went to see Lamadiere in Luganville to explain that they now wanted the church to be built. On their return they planted a church at the village of Ipayato, and not long after, the church started to spread itself to outer regions. A church was then planted at Bakataura and then Namoru. There was a school started at Keriwa on the west coast, but a dispute broke out so the school was moved to

Lalalolo. On the west coast there was a church and school started at Tcharanavusvus through Chief Ropet, who had made the request. In the same year a church was started at Nachara with the help of the landowner Joepeter.

In 1980 a church and school was planted in Passa and later transferred to a place called Mataloi. In 1992 a church was planted at Valape with a request from a man called Vareapos. In 1996 a chief called Vivirou wanted a church and school at the village of Vunakariakara in Big Bay Bush. In 2002 a church was planted in Vavuro at the request of the chief, Sunglass. Around 1980 the church had extended to Port Vila near Mel Coffee, and in 1985 onto the island of Tanna. On Tanna the church and school was planted in the village of Iatukune at the request of Chief William Nanua, who had given his land.

Organisational structure of the church

This section on the structure of the Evangelical Protestant Church does not set down the supreme rules or laws of the church; the rules are only to guide and protect the doctrine of the church and to conserve the spirit of the church's life.

Goal and aim of the church

The principal aims of this church are to bring more lost souls to Jesus Christ, to support and develop missionary work in Vanuatu, to show love in different areas of its work, to give strong support to the school (FELP), to develop youth movements and to be involved in evangelism and preaching of the gospel.

The Committee Directeur's work

The work of this committee is to call the meetings such as Union, Conferences and Campaigns; to look after the people to see that they follow the laws that the General Assembly has adopted; to watch over and use wisely the money according to the budget; to be notified of any requests from a station for support (for example, for an evangelism campaign, a religious day, opening of the church or school – the Committee Directeur must first be informed); to oversee the responsibility for the pastors, elders and deacons to look after the church; to make important decisions about the oversight of the church (for example, appoint the pastor or elder, resignation, relation with other churches); to grant leave to the pastor, accept or refuse resignations, restore the rights any pastor or elder who has been disciplined; to be the legal administrator for all the properties of the evangelical Protestant church (for example, mission ground, church and school); and to take responsibility for the spiritual formation of the members of the church including the organisation of courses in

Bible study, youth fellowship, Sunday school, women's club, and Blue Cross.

Any member of the Committee Directeur who wants to resign must give a letter of resignation to that body three months before a General Assembly.

Work of the local church

The pastor of the district and village is responsible to guide and direct every activity of the local church, with the support of the elders, deacons and teachers of each village. In the church of each village there must be worship on Sunday morning (Sunday school for children), a worship service for everyone, and the evening service to close the day. In each village there must be a youth group and men's activity. During the week there must be a prayer meeting and a Bible study (Acts 2:42; Hebrews 10:25). In each term there must be a district meeting for pastors, elders, deacons, teachers and committees of the school to discuss any problems or activities of each local school and the church (regional session).

A person who wants to become God's servant

Any person who wants to become God's servant must have a vocation (Acts 6:3).

Pastor's ordination

A person can be ordained to be a pastor if he is married and has done some courses in a Bible school. He must do two years practical work in his church as a student pastor. An elder can be promoted to become a pastor according to progress made in his work. The ordination service can be held either at the time of the general conference or at a Christian feast of the church. The person ordained must make his public promise in the church, with his family.

Duration of service

A pastor must work for two years minimum in one station. After this period the Committee Directeur can extend his time or choose another place following the request of the stations.

The condition of a pastor's job

The Committee Directeur appoints the pastor in the station that needs and asks for a pastor. Any pastor who wants a rest must submit his request to the Committee Directeur three months before the date of rest. The decision about retirement of a pastor is up to the Committee Directeur.

Good behaviour

Pastors, elders, evangelists, teachers of the church and school teachers are expected to display good behaviour.

Dedication of children (Matthew 19:13–15)

Dedication of children must take place at a Christian feast of the church (General Assembly, Easter, Pentecost Day) and on any time when a pastor visits. It is the responsibility of the parents to take the child to the pastor to bless and the congregation must support it. The pastor must be clear about the difference between dedication and baptism of children.

Baptism (Romans 6:1–6)

Baptism must be done by the Pastor (Acts 2:38–41). Before baptism can be done, the pastor or elder must be sure that those who will be baptised must first repent and really know what baptism means. Any man or woman who has accepted Christ as their personal saviour can be baptised. After the baptism the pastor gives a baptismal certificate and records the name in the local church baptism record. Only an adult can be baptised, not children.

Repentance (Acts 17:30; 1 John 1:9)

Repentance is a part of worship. After the message of the gospel is preached, the preacher must challenge his listeners about their need to repent. The church asks for public repentance or for secret repentance.

Lord's Supper (Luke 22:14–20; 1 Corinthians 1:23–24)

Every last Sunday of the month, the Lord's Supper should be taken if possible, depending on a pastor's visit. The pastor must first hold a meeting on Saturday with the leaders before the Sunday of the Lord's Supper to solve any problems between them. Only men, women, boys and girls who truly believe and accept Christ as their Saviour can part take in the Lord's Supper. They must first be baptised. The pastor must explain the meaning of the Lord's Supper to the members of his church. Anyone who takes the Lord's Supper must take it seriously (1 Corinthians 11:27–30). If any person has made a good witness but did not join in the Lord Supper, the pastor and elder must help him or her. Any couple who did not have their marriage in the church are not allowed to take part in the Lord's Supper.

Marriage (Genesis 2:21–24)

For any couple who are not married, the pastor or elder must lead them in a study of Christian marriage. Marriage must be made by any pastor for whom the Assembly has approved their name and the Ministry of Home Affairs or government has approved their nomination. The church must give clear teaching about Christian marriage. The pastor does the marriage for the couple who have been receiving the teaching about Christian marriage, and have accepted his conditions. The couple must also have been baptised. The marriage must take place in the husband's church. The pastor must record every marriage that happens in the local church, with the church's certificate and the government certificate. It is permissible to marry anyone from another church. There is no divorce. If there is a marriage problem the church must try to solve it and unite the couple again (Mark 10:2–9).

Discipline (1 Corinthians 4:19)

God's rule for his church is the Bible. If the pastor, elder, evangelist or Christian members fall into sin, the committee of discipline must consider the matter (Matthew 18:15–18). Do not give sin a chance to grow in the Assembly and church of God. We must allow God to clean the church (1 Corinthians 5:3–8). If a member or Christian brother falls, he must repent and ask forgiveness for his sin. If a Christian brother falls into sin, but does not repent, the pastor or elder must talk to him and help him (James 5:20; 1 Corinthians 6:7–8).

Categories of the punishment for Christians with discipline periods are as follows:

[Insert Table]

With any special case the Committee Directeur will consider it and make a decision.

Bible study

Any member of the church who wants to follow any Bible study course must first seek agreement from the Committee Directeur. The central cash fund of the church will be responsible for the finance. The local church also can take the responsibility for finance, if possible, or individual people can be responsible for finance. The church cannot be responsible for any student who does the Bible study but does not have the agreement of the Committee Directeur of the church or General Assembly.

Visit (Outreach – *Kerisiano*) (Matthew 28:19)

Kerisiano is a visit that the church does once a year. The aim of the visit is to wake up the village to the Christian life (elders, Christian workers); for encouragement; to show that the church is always thinking about them; to hear the local news of their work; look for decisions to carry out; and check on baptism, marriage, and Blue Cross. Involved in the visit must be one pastor, one elder and two other Christians. The district must form a team for the visit; one team for Santo, one for west coast Malekula, and one for east coast

Malekula. Those whose team cannot visit their own places must exchange, for example, Santo people must go to Malekula and Malekula people to Santo. If there are needs, questions or problems found by any team that are hard to handle, they must submit them to the Committee Directeur to consider. If any team reaches any village where there are some Christians who have fallen, it is time to lift them up and put them back into the ministry. These visits are not for politics, but for spiritual purposes only.

Religious campaign

Local or overseas evangelists of other churches who want to hold crusades in any village of the Protestant mission must first have the agreement of the Committee Directeur of the church. If any local or overseas evangelist wants to make campaigns in any Protestant village with the spirit of division (to start another church), the chief, pastor or elder must not let him in.

Work inside the village

All villages must participate in every activity for the school, including building classrooms and other houses, or work that the Committee of FELP asks to be done. In the village, the Session and district must cooperate to build classrooms, churches or the pastor's house. Help can come from the central cash fund if there is need. For any major work, a local church must make a request to the General Assembly. Every problem must be solved before any work takes place.

Finance

The payment of the workmen of the FELP for whom the Government is not responsible will be the responsibility of the administrative Director and Committee who will fix an amount as a salary for them. The payment of the pastor is up to the village or the General Assembly to decide. For the payment of the pastor and elder who stay in their own village, the General Assembly will decide. If a pastor, elder or evangelist has any job in Government or a private company and has a salary, the church will help them only when there is need.

Overseas tours

The General Conference of the church or the Committee Directeur can choose one, two or more members of the church to represent the church in any general conference of the church outside the country (overseas), and also can ask help from other countries for financial support.

The funeral

It is the job of the pastor, elder, deacon and evangelist to bury a person. If a leader of the church dies, it is good to call a pastor to bury him, to invite any authority nearby to attend, and also to pass the news of death by message on radio. To bury a person from another church, there must be an agreement from their Committee first. Before burying a person, if possible wait a day (24 hours). The burial service is held according to the wishes of the family, most commonly in the church, otherwise in the house or at the cemetery.

The leader who wants to become a politician

Before any pastor, elder or deacon can be a candidate in a political party they must first ask for leave of three months. Every member of the church must do something good for the country. We believe that as servants of God, we must do God's will; 'Give the things for Caesar to Caesar; and the things for God to God'. As servants of God, we are responsible for the souls of the people.

General Assembly

At the end of every year there is an annual conference (called Synod) of the church in the month of December, held normally in Santo or Malekula. The conference will choose the place that will host the next synod, in the ceremonial rite at the end of the conference. Every pastor, elder, executive committee member of the church, teacher and one committee member of the school of each village, must attend the conference. A village can also nominate some normal members of the church to go to the conference. The representative of each church must come to participate in the synod. Synod has approved a 500-vatu contribution for each delegate.

Amendment

Any amendment in these structures and rules can be made by a three-quarter majority of the members in the General Conference (Synod). The proposals must first be submitted to the Committee Directeur to study, and a copy must be given to each of the three districts. (North West and North East Malekula and South Santo) three months before the General Assembly.

The procedure for nomination of the members of the Committee Directeur and FELP

In the past, the nomination for the position of members has come directly at the Synod by adopting the normal procedure of election. To make the members of the church serious about their responsibilities in the school and church, any member who refuses to attend two consecutive General Synods will not participate in any vote or election for the membership of both Committees Directeur, but he can attend the Synod as an observer. The Synod will never accept this delegate to be a candidate for new nomination.

149

Causes of religious tension

Here we shall look at some of what I consider are the sources of the religious tension within the Protestant Church in Vanuatu. According to my personal observation and understanding as a member of the Protestant Church, there are some things that I think are major problems in the life of my church today.

Island-ism

One of the big problems today in the church is Island-ism. Island-ism means to favour people from your island and give them a job ahead of someone from outside who is more qualified or suitable. This is a very bad attitude to apply in the church. I see most politicians and government officials always apply it. There is tension in the Solomon Islands between Guadalcanal and Malaita because of Island-ism and now it has come into the church that is the Body of Christ. This brings tension and division within the family of God. The application of Island-ism in the Protestant Church is a really big issue. For example, one man might want people only from Malekula to work with him in the office, even if the people he wants do not know the purpose of this office. Their aim is simply to occupy places in the office, but for what benefit? The same is true in Santo.

This problem paralyses our church today because people never share the work between the two islands, and do not work together to establish the Kingdom of God. Both groups never have a common thought on any matter; they always disagree about their decision-making and the work in the church, and they criticise each other. It is Island-ism that is influencing them, and it creates tension and division in the church. Today this tension within the Protestant Church in Vanuatu is really strong and has resulted in a split between the groups.

Qualifications and quality of the leaders

The matter of qualifications and quality of leaders has played a big role in the life of our church. We need talented people to lead the church to achieve its purposes and this requires certain qualifications and qualities. Today the Protestant Church is in need. There are no qualified leaders who are well trained in the Word of God so that they can lead the church at the present time. Those who are in leadership positions do not teach what the Bible has set for Christians to follow. They lead people according to their own earthly wisdom.

In the section above on the organisational structure of our church, it rightly states that to be a leader a person needs to enter a Bible school to learn the Word of God. It also states that a person needs to spend years gaining practical experience and then enter the ministry. But the serious problem in the Protestant Church today is that these rules are not followed. The church ordains people to be pastors and elders who have never had any theological training; these men have almost no knowledge of the Word of God. So I think the lack of a good theological education means the leaders do not know where to lead the people.

Apart from theological training, we also need leaders who have certain qualities, for example, they must have some years of experience in the work of the church. The failure of my church is that they choose people who are young and have no experience in the church before they take up the role of leadership. Because of the problem of lack of experience the church cannot function as well as it should.

Meeting procedures

Tension within the Protestant Church in Vanuatu also shows up in the General Synod. This happens because the people who chair the meetings do not know how to control them. This was certainly true in the time of the General Synod that I attended. Many conflicts arose because the members did not have any meeting procedure guidelines that they could follow to make sure that that everything went well in the meeting. I remember, for example, the tension that was created because some people forced others to vote for a particular person in the election of a new board. This practice is against the rules of meeting, but the person chairing did not stop it. There are many more examples.

Decision-making in the church

There is a big problem in making decisions in the church. The reason I say this is because during my attendance at one particular general meeting, I realised that there was a lot of confusion in the process of making decisions. There were non-Christians, those who never attended the church, together with some politicians, who joined the meeting of the church, and took part in decision-making and the running of the church. This is totally against the Word of God. Their ideas are very different from those of Christians. They always make wrong decisions because they do not know nor follow the Word of God.

Another problem I observed in the General Synod meeting I attended was that there were two meetings being held at the same time: one for FELP (education) and the other for the church. When this happens it leads to mass confusion in the meetings, because the church members take part in the decision-making of education. Education members in their turn take part in the decision-making of the church. This leads to confusion and bad decisions. Everything is like Tanna soup (a mixture of ideas and thoughts) and if we keep on going in this way, our church will end up in bankruptcy and tumult.

Separation of church from education and politics

I think that the idea of Charlemagne (the founder of the Free Protestant Church) to put politics, education and church all together as one must be changed. It causes tensions, not because of the doctrinal differences, but because FELP leaders and other leaders all fight to get the better positions within their respective groups. For this reason, I suggest that there should be a committee and General Synod for FELP by itself, for the church by itself, and for the FMP political party by itself.

Pride and disobedience

Some tensions in the church should have been resolved soon after they began, but because of pride and disobedience to the Word of God the tension and division still remains today. I remember one occasion when a particular fight began. The old people in the village of Namoru wanted to resolve it through the methods of traditional custom. However it did not work out this way because some of the church leaders did not want to humble themselves; these leaders did not want someone to correct them, and were not willing to change their opinions. I think it was pride and disobedience in their hearts that prevented them, resulting in the tension remaining till this day.

Theological reflections: The church and the Bible

We need to study carefully what the Bible says about the church: how it should function, what kind of people should be in leadership roles, how to run the church meeting, and so on. The Bible is the only guide and rule for us as Christians and we should seek and heed its advice.

The word 'church' comes from the Greek word *ecclesia*, which means 'an assembly of people called out'. The visible church is an assembly who meet in the name of the Lord Jesus for prayer, thanksgiving, breaking of bread, and the preaching and teaching of God's Word. The real purpose of the church is set down in Ephesians 4:12–13: 'for the perfecting of the saints, for the work of the ministry, for the edifying of the body of Christ: Till we all come in the unity of the faith, and of the knowledge of the Son of God, to a perfect humanity, to the measure of the stature of the fullness of Christ'.

As we study the four Gospels and Acts, we will find out about the church and its workings. We can say that the first church that was local and visible existed in the time of Jesus Christ and consisted of Christ and the apostles. This church community had its own pastor (John 10:11–14) and a treasurer (John 13:29). It also did missionary work (Matthew 10:1–11) and baptised those who believed (John 4:1–2). It was instructed about disciplining (Matthew 18:15–17), observed the Lord's Supper (Matthew 25:26–28) and sang hymns (Hebrews 2:12).

Acts 1:12–14 presents a good model of how the church should be. On the basis of this text, I would like to set down some important things about the church.

The church and the role of a pastor (Acts 1:12–14)

The early church assembled to praise God (Acts 1:12). According to Luke 24:52–53, the disciples were no longer afraid but rejoiced in what God was about to do. They assembled in an upper room (Acts 1:13a): this shows that the church must meet in a local place. There were pastors (1:13b): the apostles served as pastors in the church at Jerusalem. There were people who joined the assembly (1:14–15): the membership of this first church was about 120, including the apostles, the women, Mary, and James, the Lord's half-brother. They assembled to pray (1:14): this showed their obedience to the Word of the God.

We consider these things keys for success in the Lord's work. As mentioned above, in such an organisation there is a chief who looks after everything, so that all things are done in the right way. By 'chief' I refer to pastors, deacons and church leaders. These spiritual leaders play a huge part in the life of the church. A pastor's work is extremely important as he is called to be a spiritual leader for the people. His ministry is to bring people from darkness to light, hopelessness to hopefulness, sadness to joy, from a slave to Satan to the power of God, which means bringing someone from death to life eternal. The people will listen to his preaching, teaching and advice, and they will call on him in time of trouble and difficulty. The pastor should be the leader of his flock, the power of the weak, the guide of the ignorant, and the friend of the sinner.

Conduct of church business meetings

Ezekiel 34:4 says: 'The diseased you have not strengthened, neither have you healed the sick; you have not bound up the broken, neither have you brought back those who were driven away, you have not sought out the lost; but with force and with cruelty have you ruled them.'

This verse is an accusation against the false shepherds of Israel and a call to faithful servant leadership for the Lord. In the New Testament, the apostle Paul himself sets out a good list of criteria for church leadership in 1 Timothy 3:1–7. It is worth noting the following from this text:

> If a man desire the office of leadership, he desires a good work. A church leader must be blameless, the husband of one wife, vigilant, sober, of good behaviour, given to

hospitality, apt to teach. He is not given to wine, not greedy for money; he is patient, not a brawler, not covetous. He is one who rules well his own house, and his children obey him, for if he does not know how to rule his own house then how can he take care of the church of God? He is not a novice, lest being lifted up with pride he falls into the condemnation of the devil; moreover he must have a good rapport with those who are without lest he fall into reproach and the snare of the devil.

When we look at Acts 1:15–28, we find out about the business of the church. In this passage we have the report of the church meeting to find a replacement for Judas Iscariot. Here we learn some very important principles on how to conduct a scriptural business meeting. It is the job of the pastor to call and control the meeting. In verse 15, it was Peter, the leading pastor among the apostles, and the first pastor committed to the care of the sheep (John 21:15–17) who raised the matter for consideration. The call and control of church business should come from those that God has appointed to a leadership position. (See also Acts 5:2, 15:4, 13, 19, 22.) Any church business meeting must have some biblical purpose (v.16). Many problems have come about because churches hold business meetings just for the sake of holding them.

At any meeting of God's people there needs to be a clear purpose, that is, 'The Scripture must be fulfilled'. This is the basis of any business meeting. Acts 1:21–22 shows us the leadership of the pastor. If we observe carefully we can see there are three elements to scriptural church government: the rule of Christ, the head (Ephesians 1:22–23; Colossians 1:18); the rule of the pastor, the 'under shepherd' (1 Timothy 5:17); and the rule of the church, the congregation (Matthew 18:17). The pastor's job is to give the church guidance before it makes any decision. Like Peter here, he instructs the people about what to vote for, not who to vote for (see also Acts 6:3). In this case, the two men proposed as candidates were equally qualified (Acts 1:23). Many churches have put men into positions, not because they were qualified, but because there was a vacancy that had to be filled. Acts 1:24-26 shows us that only through prayer can the church find out the will of God. The church must pray about every matter proposed in the business meeting so that they might make the right decision according to God's will.

Personal interpretation

We have already looked at the causes of religious tension in the previous pages. Most of them were not caused by the congregation, but by the church government and spiritual leaders. However, let us direct our attention back to the beginning of creation and the story of Adam and Eve. This will remind us that we cannot blame the church government and the spiritual leaders alone. Both are good, but there is the problem of sin in the world, which came through our ancestors Adam and Eve. This is the source of every problem that humankind, including both the church leaders and the congregation, must face.

When we look in the Bible at the history of Israel, it teaches us another very important lesson. First of all, God chose Israel to be a holy nation and told them that God would be their king. But the Israelites disobeyed God and rejected him. They wanted a human king like other nations, one who could lead them into battle. This meant they did not trust God any more to fight for them, but wanted to trust a man – the king who would lead them. God was angry with them but gave them a king. In the end, it resulted in destruction, division among the Israelites and fighting for positions (to be king). The same will be true of the church that lets humans govern by their own understanding and without Christ – the result will be destruction. The church will not function well, there will be division in the church, fighting for positions, and this will ruin the body of Christ. We know that the church is the body of Christ, therefore we need to put Christ as the head of the church and also of our own lives. Only through Christ can we accomplish his purpose.

Pastoral approach

The only way that we can solve our problems and correct our mistakes is through the Word of God, the Bible. It is the only source of guidance and direction in everything we do. Paul himself said in 2 Timothy 3:16; 17:16, 'All Scripture is given by the inspiration of God, and is profitable for doctrine, for reproof, for correction, for instruction in righteousness: that the man of God may be perfect, thoroughly furnished in all good works'.

Everything in this essay is about those who want to take up the role of leadership in the church. This is because, according to my own understanding, most of the problems in the church come from the leaders. If the leader is good, then the church will function well, but if the leader is bad then the church will be paralysed. Consider the nation of Israel: if the king was corrupt, the whole nation was affected; it reaped the consequences of the king's sin. I think it is the same for the church. For this reason I think that if we solve the problem of providing good leaders of the church, then through this, most problems in the church can be solved.

Essentials

Born again

The first and most essential thing is that a man must be 'born again'. Before a person starts any work for the Lord, he must have firm assurance that he is a child of God (John 3:3). A man is born again when he confesses to God that he is a sinner and realises that Jesus, the Lamb of God, died for him, and he receives Christ into his heart. Being born of God, a man is then a new creation (2 Corinthians 5:17).

The call of God

The pastor or leader must be called by God. Paul introduces his first letter to the Corinthians with these words: 'Paul, called to be an apostle' (see also Acts 22:14–15). For Paul, the call of God was more precious than life itself. When a man receives the call of God it changes the orientation of his whole life. If any one wants to be a leader and involved in the ministry, but does not receive this call, he cannot do anything in the ministry (note Acts 20:24). Every leader must receive the call of God.

Confirmation of the call

If a man's call is truly by God, God will reveal this to his servants to whom he gave the responsibility to direct the church. In the early church, God spoke to those who were responsible by the Holy Spirit saying, 'Set apart Barnabas and Saul for the work where I have called them' (Acts 13:2). Barnabas and Paul received the call of God in their heart and this call was confirmed, and they were recognised in the church. God himself will open the way and will confirm a person's call. The Holy Spirit is our counsellor. A person must obey the Holy Spirit's voice and follow what he says. This way he will work in harmony with other servants and with the rest of the body of Christ. I emphasise the call of God because I believe that many pastors and church leaders have not been called of God. They just want to be involved in the ministry because of a vacancy, or perhaps they just want the job. They do not do good work, they lead the church in the wrong way; disputes arise and sometimes this leads to division. Why is this? I think it is because these leaders are not called by God.

Qualifications

To be involved in the ministry there are certain steps of preparation I consider to be very important for any church leader. Those who want to take on the role of leadership must go through them. These steps can be summarised under the two headings of Qualifications and Qualities.

A good understanding of the Word of God.

Before a man can preach, it is necessary to have a good understanding of the Word of God. Paul went into Arabia (Galatians 1:17); this was almost certainly to study the Word of God. Jesus knew well the Scriptures and cited them often. Paul himself said to Timothy, 'Study to show yourself approved by God, a workman that needs not to be ashamed, rightly dividing the word of truth'.

Biblical training

Because it is necessary to know and understand the Word of God, a person needs to undertake some Bible courses (which look at the whole Bible). This is to familiarise himself with the Scriptures so he can cite it in his messages. Such study gives him some ideas that he can use in his preaching. The pastor and leader should love and honour the Word of God; it is his adviser, it is his daily guide, it feeds his hungry soul, it is the seed that spreads into his mission field.

Qualities

Not only does a man of God need to know the Word of God, but he must also have certain qualities. These qualities can only be obtained through experience. This experience can be gained from someone who has had many experiences. With these qualities he can lead the church well and his ministry will be successful. Just as the quality of fruit depends upon the tree, so too the ministry of a pastor or leader depends on his character. The bad tree cannot produce good fruit.

Love

Love must be one of the greatest qualities in the life of the Christian leader. Without love he cannot win any souls and please God. Love must fill his life. He must love his family. He must love the members of his assembly. He must love the young people. He must love non-Christians to bring them to Christ.

Holiness

The Christian leader or pastor must live a holy life. He must always tell the truth. He must be honest. He must not use or listen to swearing. He must be prudent in his behaviour with every person of the opposite sex. To be the light of the Lord shining in the dark he must win the confidence and the respect of the community.

Courage

The pastor or Christian leader needs courage to preach the gospel because he will face much opposition. He must be faithful when people are against him. John the Baptist had no fear to say to the Governor, 'You are not allowed to have your brother's wife'. When proclaiming God's word a pastor must not be afraid to expose sin and take measures against the members of the church who continue to sin.

Zeal in the work

The Christian leader must be zealous in his work. It is not right to stay in bed while the members of the church get up early to go to work. God himself says that he gets up early to talk to his prophets and send them (Jeremiah 25:3–4). This shows that the prophets get up early like God – in the first hour of the day. This is the best time for prayer and personal study in the Word of God. Early in the morning a man can prepare his preaching and plan his daily work. The Christian leader must be active in visiting the members of his church. Jesus said to pray that the master would send forth labourers (workmen) into his harvest field, not those that are lazy (Matthew 9:38).

Faith

The pastor must be a man of faith. He must exercise his faith by believing that God will help him in each project. Faith makes everything possible, but unbelief steals all blessing. By his spirit of faith, the pastor will train his congregation to have confidence in him and follow him.

The spirit of prayer

The prayer life of a pastor cannot be emphasised enough. The people who accomplish great things for God are those who understand the importance of prayer. The man of God must ask God to give him a heart that has a burden for the salvation of souls, healing for the sick, and so on. The pastor must learn to seek God in prayer and praise until he can reach the throne. Then he can see God open the windows of heaven and pour out blessings upon him and his congregation.

Patience

The pastor or Christian leader must be a man of great patience. 1 Thessalonians 5:14 says, 'Now we exhort you, brethren, warn them that are unruly, comfort the feebleminded, support the weak, be patient toward all'. To be patient means to be slow in anger and not to let out strong words from your mouth when you are angry. Ephesians 4:32 says, 'And be kind one to another, tender-hearted, forgiving one another, even as God for Christ's sake hath forgiven you'.

Conclusion

I hope that what I have written in this paper gives you some enlightenment and helpful guidance about the cause of tensions in the Protestant Church of Vanuatu, and how they might be overcome. In particular I hope that it is clear as to how a Christian leader should behave and lead their church. We must discard what is bad and keep what is good according to the Word of God. We must then apply it to our ministry to lead our people into maturity of faith in Christ. My prayer is that the Lord will help each of us to lead his church for his glory.

Bibliography

The Holy Bible, King James Version

Bourke, F. H, *Le Pasteur Fidèle*, Lausanne Suisse: Imprimerie de Valency, 1994 Place: publisher

Manwo, Pastor Jimmy & Rabty, Jean, *Structure blong Eglise Libre*, Place: publisher, 2000

Tamumu, Pastor Ajapunja, *Mission Protestante de Nouvelle Calédonie aux Nouvelles Hébrides*, Place: publisher, 1985

Youth Decline in the Presbyterian Church of Vanuatu

Graham Path

Introduction

The National Youth Convention held in July 2002 at Magam village on the island of Ambrym dealt with the issue of the Presbyterian Church and Youth in Vanuatu, in particular the question, 'How does the Presbyterian Church of Vanuatu understand the problems of youth in the light of the membership decline (according to church statistics)?'

The issue of the decline of youth membership in the Presbyterian Church was mentioned also in a message from the Coordinator of the National Youth of the Presbyterian Church in 2002. He said that the church has inherited much from the past, both from the Presbyterian (church) and Melanesian (cultural) traditions, and that the church has to combine these together in order to give strength and meaning to the youth and their worship.

Youth Ministry has been in the Presbyterian Church for many years and has provided activities and programs at congregational level as follows: Sunday School, Youth Fellowship, Boy Scouts, Girl's Brigade and Girl Guides. The programs later provided for combined youth and Sunday school, where several congregations came together once a month to have slightly larger groups. The strength of these programs is the regular weekly meeting of the core group to arrange activities and make decisions. But again there are weaknesses because there is no leadership training, no policy guidelines and no directions. Also, every branch of the youth was working in isolation. There was no combined Session, Presbytery or National Youth network.

The National Youth Convention brought all our youth leaders together and in 2002 the National Sunday School convention brought all our Sunday school teachers together. This has enabled all our youth and Sunday school leaders to train and have fellowship together. The service delivery to all our youth is now better but needs committed pastors, elders, deacons and other leaders to support the structure. The structure is as follows:

[Insert Diagram]

The youth program is described as a 'holistic ministry' because the activities that are carried out are taken from the youth's Four Square Program and covers all aspects of life:

1. Spiritual (devotional) – to do with our relationship with God; the aim is worship, spiritual growth and maturity, and individual and community discipleship.
2. Social (recreational) – to do with our relationship with other people; the aim is Christian fellowship and unity, enjoyment and fun, and physical development and fitness.
3. Educational – to do with the development of our thinking and with learning new skills (to go hand in hand with the knowledge of God); the aim is ongoing development of knowledge and skills, and application of Christian principles to everyday life.
4. Service – to do with our commitment to the church and our wider community; the aim is to provide opportunities to give practical help to others as a community witness for Christ.[92]

Despite these activities for the youth in our churches today, the youth numbers are declining in our Presbyterian Church congregations. Why is this so? We need to reconsider this question seriously. Therefore I have divided this paper into sections that I think will help us to understand the reasons.

I decided to write about this issue because I was once a leader of the youth in my village in Hog Harbour and in my Session, and a member of the executive for youth in Santo Presbytery. When I attended the National Youth Convention at Mele, the reports from each Presbytery showed that there was a decline in numbers. Again in 2002, when the Youth Convention was held, the Presbytery reports showed that there was continuing decline.

As a youth leader and now a pastoral student in Talua, I think we need to solve this issue because I believe that our youth are the future leaders in our society, our churches and our country. Without a spiritual knowledge about God, youth will not give leadership at the standard that we in our church expect. From my research I have come to understand that the issue of the decline of youth membership in the church is nationwide; it applies to all denominations of the church. However, in my paper I am only referring to the Presbyterian Church of Vanuatu, and especially in the rural areas.

I was able to gather some information through my interviews with young people who attended the 2002 National Youth Convention held at Magam village in Ambrym, and with pastors, elders and youth who live in rural areas.

Brief background of the relationship between church and youth

Structure

There is a very strong structural relationship between the Youth Organisation and the General Assembly of the Presbyterian Church. The youth structure is part of the Assembly structure and decisions made by the youth follow the same procedure as decisions by other parts of the Assembly. The General Assembly makes the final decisions on all important matters. This shows that there is a very strong relationship between the two. Whatever decision is recommended by the youth executive to Assembly and agreed by the Assembly is then passed on to the congregations. Each of the two organisations work hand in hand to help build the church and spread the gospel. With this good relationship, they also help each other to carry out each other's activities.

Youth and Church Structures

[Insert Diagram]

Constitution

Both the Youth and the General Assembly have their own constitutions that guide their actions. In the Assembly constitution, under the heading 'Building up the Christian and Witness', it provides a means by which the church might have a good relationship with youth:

> The session shall arrange for all parish members to be involved in their work, learning and witnessing to Jesus Christ as Lord and Saviour. It shall encourage all members to worship regularly, encourage Christian life in the home, and cope with any special needs which arise. It shall arrange and endorse the work of Sunday school, Bible study, Prayer life, PWMU [Presbyterian Women's Missionary Union], Youth Group, Confirmation classes, stewardship and evangelism.
> (*Presbyterian Church of Vanuatu Constitution*, p. 12, 5:2.6)

The Youth Working Policy is under the heading 'Power of Youth Decision' (p. 2):
a. Neither the PYG [Presbyterian Youth Group] nor the PYFG [Presbyterian Youth Fellowship Group] has the right or power on its own to make decisions without session or presbytery approval.
b. Neither the PYG nor the PYFG shall make any decision in any form or in anyway to disturb the authority of the Session or the

Presbytery.

c. The PYFG or PYG is to be a loyal servant of the Session and Presbytery.

Through the structures and constitutions of the church it is clear that the church and the youth have or very strong relationship, both spiritual and physical. So why is the youth membership of the church declining?

The concept of youth as perceived by Presbyterians in Vanuatu

When we talk about a definition of youth in the Vanuatu context there is a wide range of understandings of who this means. The view of Presbyterians in Vanuatu is the same as the Western view, namely that the term 'youth' refers to the group of people usually aged between the 13 and 26 years. The youth are the group of people between childhood and adulthood. These are the people that I think the church needs to reconsider, because youth are so important in our society and especially in the church today.

According to the statistics for Vanuatu, in the year 1999, Vanuatu's total population was 177,370. In the category of 0-9 years there were 56,758, which is equal to 32 percent; 10-24 years there were 54,984, which is equal to 31 percent; over 24 years there were 65,628, which is equal to 37 percent. In other words, 31 percent of Vanuatu's population were in the youth age group.

Youth in our church are very important and need reconsidering because:

- Youth form a large percentage of the population inside and outside of the church.
- Youth are the future of the church.
- Youth have a big contribution to share with the church and community.
- Youth are future leaders for our church, nation and community.
- Youth is a time of many new challenges and problems, a time of many changes in life and culture.
- Youth is a time of formation so they need training, teaching and instruction.
- Youth have lots of energy and are interested in doing things.
- Youth need companionship with other Christian youth and encouragement in Christian values.[93]

So if we want our church to develop physically and spiritually, and if we want to stop the youth decline in our church, we need to have a good knowledge of the special needs, challenges and problems that young people are experiencing. We need to understand that youth is a time of change from immaturity to maturity, from dependence to independence, from childhood to adulthood.

Youth in the past and their problems

Long before the foreigners (meaning planters, traders and missionaries) brought changes into our islands, especially in the rural areas, the early youth spent all their time in their villages learning all they had to know about their custom ways of living and behaving. Their custom and cultural ways of doing things was their only education. They had no organisation as a youth fellowship, but served under the leadership of their chief. They were obedient and respectful to their parents and leaders of their villages. This cultural education taught them well and prepared them for future responsibilities as leaders. Everyone in the village had to do what the leaders of the village required. Everyone worked as a team to help educate the youth.

Through this teamwork, the respect and obedience shown by the youth to the leaders of the village, and especially to the chief, helped to give the youth advice and to teach them in the following ways to:
- Be involved and participate fully in the community work and social activities such as marriage ceremonies, death, feasting, dancing, and so on.
- Have strong cultural beliefs and fear of sacred places, so that if youth did not obey or respect, they would face a heavy discipline.
- Have respect for the cultural way of life.
- Learn to accept correction and be reconciled.
- Have respect for their families and other people.[94]

Therefore youth in the past did not have as much freedom of choice as they have today, but inside their hearts, they knew that someone cared for them and protected them. Some of the skills that the youth practiced at home included custom ceremonies, caring of animals, hunting of wild animals and birds, and fishing. Boys learned from their fathers, while girls learned from their mothers. Both boys and girls learned to weave bamboo, as well as to plant crops in the garden at certain times of the year, and the times to harvest them. Culturally, cooperation that involved obedience and respect was part of the upbringing of youth. They did all things in common and shared ideas about their skills. There was no ill feeling, as they developed ideas together. For that reason youth put their whole heart into learning and doing what they could do.

When referring to youth in this context we are talking about a community where everyone is involved in custom ceremonies, village projects and much more. In the past, youth was not described by age but by appearance. The old people chose who the youth leaders would be, then they took the time and responsibility to teach and instruct the chosen ones for the particular work of leadership. To be chosen as a leader in the past was a respectful responsibility, so the young leader needed to learn all he could for the important task ahead of him. All the members respected, honoured and cooperated with him in the great task.

But then the arrival of foreigners, especially the missionaries with their teachings and Western culture, affected the youth. There was ill feeling between those who lived in heathenism and those who accepted Christianity; between those who were educated and those who were not educated; between those who were rich and those who were poor. With these new teachings the youth developed a new way of learning that began and has continued to bring confusion between their cultural values and Western values.[95]

These teachings led the youth to forget respect and obedience to custom values, to develop individualism in their minds, and to lose their strong commitment to their families. It also led to a fading away of the law and order once enjoyed, and to youth moving out of the village for education and work in the towns.

The introduction of these teachings has affected the youth up until today and it has especially brought a strong spirit of individualism. For this reason it is very easy for youth numbers to decline in the church, because the youth are free to disobey church regulations. But then we ask the question, What has the church done to stop youth numbers declining? There is not much for the youth to do on Sundays except to be involved with people who go to worship, and if their parents allow them, to join studies and other activities organised by the ministers.

If we refer back to the time before the missionaries came in 1848, the youth lived under the leadership and guidance of parents and leaders of the village. The youth were not regarded as youth as they are today, but they were regarded as men who could help out during tribal wars and were able to do what men were expected to do in the village. The missionaries who came never thought of separating the youth from the chiefs' organisations, so the youth continued to have a good working relationship with the community. While the youth helped out with all the usual activities, the missionaries were busy setting up mission stations, building churches, evangelising and, most of all, finding ways of overcoming the challenges of traditional beliefs. Therefore, in those days, youth were not considered important by the missionaries. Also at that time the missionaries were trying their best to educate the people, whether younger or older, to be able to spread the message of the gospel. In that sense, youth were important, but the idea of starting a youth fellowship was impossible.[96]

Challenges of contemporary youth

Since the missionaries came there has been a decline in the traditional education that once made the lives of New Hebrideans rich and meaningful. So the church had to do something to enrich the lives of the people again. For this reason, around the year 1900, the missionaries introduced their own type of education, called adult education. It consisted of Bible study, reading, writing, counting and singing. In 1895, the church established its own educational institution called Teachers Training Institute (TTI), then changed it to a Bible College in 1971. The church also developed other institutions, for example, Onesua High School and various district schools.

By the year 1953, the church thought it was a good idea to start up a youth ministry (Fifth Session of General Assembly, minute 68). In 1957, the Assembly agreed to establish a youth ministry under the supervision of missionaries (Ninth General Assembly, minute 21). The missionaries supervised the work of the youth fellowship until 1974, when a ni-Vanuatu named John Sethy Regenvanu, from Malekula, took over as a Christian Education Director. But due to the changes that took place when Vanuatu gained its independence in 1980, John Sethy went into politics and was replaced by Kali Vatoko. The changes of environment brought about by independence, affected youth also, so in order keep youth involved in church activities, the church introduced many activities in the youth program. The program is known as a four square program, consisting of spiritual, educational, social and service activities (as described above). The aim was to prepare the youth for their future responsibilities as wives or husbands, and as leaders of the church, the local communities and the nation, and to be good citizens of Vanuatu.

But again many things have changed. The problems today among youth are caused by the school system that teaches foreign ideas and knowledge that does not fit the youth's own society. If they had a system that was similar to the old system, they would easily cope with it, but because it is different, then it creates an atmosphere of confusion. This leads to a decline of youth in the church because young people have no money, no respect, no work and no commitment, and they do not feel responsible in the way that they did when they were taught traditional things in the past.[97]

Western ideologies were taught because it was thought that they were better than our traditional ways. The traditional ways of making houses, hunting, marriages and much more are slowly disappearing. Through the individualism emphasised through the foreign education system, youth have been encouraged to think of themselves as individuals and to disobey their parents; as a result community life has broken down.

The least number of youth in Vanuatu in any of the educational organisations or activities is in the churches. In Vanuatu each year about a quarter of the youth population takes part in some kind of youth activities and adult education program. Many youth just wander around in their villages and only a few go to church, attend Bible classes, join youth clubs, participate in discussion groups, meet with parent groups or teach in Sunday school. It seems that youth numbers are declining in church very rapidly because not enough activities provided for them. They have found that the church is a place where people come only for worship, on Sundays and other days, as part of their commitment, but it is not a place where people come to worship God with a true heart (John 4:24). Youth have found that religion is not relevant to their lives and that through the church they are not helped to relate with others as persons.

Youth are encouraged by pastors, parents, leaders of communities and people to attend church and its activities, but they find it very hard because there are also many other social activities around them that suit their interests, such as video shows, fundraising events, feasts and other entertainment. Some youth are also attracted to attend other sects because these other groups are more creative in the way in which they provide for, encourage and involve their youth.

The decline of youth in the Church today

This section sets out ideas that I have gathered from talking with people and interviewing them. I attended the Presbyterian Youth National Convention held in June 2002 and asked some questions concerning the above subject. The Central Islands Youth (CIY) and Malekula Presbytery Youth (MPY) came up with the following points:

• We think that decline of youth membership in the church is an important issue that the church needs to reconsider because it is happening in all our local Sessions, but our religious leaders are just sitting back without helping to find ways of dealing with it. If we are not careful our youth may easily find other activities that suit their own interests. Then what will happen is that they will be more interested in attending those outside activities than in attending church activities. This will continue the decline we are talking about.
• Another point is that today youth are thought of as future leaders of their nation, their communities and the church. However, without any knowledge of God, youth will not be able to perform to the standard that people deserve because they have not gained the knowledge required by our national motto, 'In God we stand'.
• The church wanted to educate youth, so it established a youth ministry in all our presbyteries. We have a very close relationship with the wider church through our working structure. Although we

have our own structure, we are supposed to be responsible to our local Session, to the Presbytery, and then to the Assembly through the Christian Education Director.

• The youth all have to follow a program called the 'Four Square Program', which consists of spiritual, social, educational and service activities. When we begin our program, it is very successful at first, but later becomes weak through the decline in youth numbers. The reason for this is that the youth leaders' faith is not stable; this then leads to further membership decline because the youth are not sure about their faith. In the meantime, the pastor is too busy concentrating on other church matters, and so the youth are lost, and in return, they ignore the church.

• Western ideas have come into our communities through education. The youth are strongly influenced by the schools, and the new teachings, which contrast with community values, lead to disrespect. They say, 'Our country is a democratic country and I am free to choose whether or not I have involvement in youth ministry and church activities; I can follow my own desires'. This clearly shows a spirit of individualism and a reason for the decline.

• In summary then, the main causes of youth decline are not enough teaching, no visitation by the pastor and Session members, unstable youth leaders, unstable church leaders, Western influences and other outside activities that better suit the youth interest. To solve the problem, youth leaders of church, Christians, people, parents and chiefs need to be united in encouraging, teaching, helping and taking part in each other's activities. But, again, without the help and guidance of God's Spirit, we cannot succeed in our plans, so the church has first of all to pray for young people, to encourage them, to teach them God's Word, and to visit them so that they will feel that they are not being left out.

• Further, the Presbytery and local Session should monitor closely the youth activities, so that if there is a problem then they can help. Because the youth are important people, they need to be cared for. Therefore we think it is very important that youth should have their own pastor in all Presbyteries to work especially with the youth, to help them to find their weakness and to improve. A lot could be achieved with proper pastoral care for the youth.

Interview with Kali Vatoko

During the 2002 General Assembly meeting, I spoke with Elder Kalo Vatoko from Mele and these are some of his responses:

• The church offers strong support for youth fellowship. The youth are regarded by the church as their sheep and youth view the church as their shepherd. Youth depend on the church for encouragement in how to prepare them as future leaders.

• The church's purpose in setting up the youth fellowship was to teach and train the youth to be good and future leaders of nation, church and society. When there is decline of youth membership it is up to the church to solve the issue because the church is the head of the youth organisation. We also have to consider the matter of youth decline because we do not want the youth to be left out of any of the church activities, because the church is their foundation and that is where they will find peace in their hearts.

• Another fact is that we leaders are the ones responsible for the decline because of we have not provided enough teaching or visitation, and we have not participated in the youth program, so we have to help solve the issue. The church is the body that the youth submit to under its regulations. Within a community and local Session, the Session is responsible for any religious activities being carried out, for example Sunday school, Sunday devotions, 10 am and 3 pm worship services. But it is sad to say that most of the time the youth have been left out because they are not included in conducting services. This is because the Session does not trust the youth. This leads to youth decline in the church, because the youth feel that they have been left out.

• Here are some further points: the youth are tired of the same people preaching at Sunday Services; there are no activities in church that suit their interest, like musical instruments for singing, educational video tapes, Bible quizzes, outreach to other churches; gossiping among church people gives a bad example to youth; leaders of the church point out youth failures without helping them; and church leaders are not stable in their leadership – the way in which they live and act does not follow what they preach and teach.

• We can only solve this problem if we commit ourselves fully to Jesus Christ. By that, I mean the youth must be filled with spiritual teachings so that they may be ready to face the challenges ahead of them. Due to changes of teaching, the church needs to insert some local knowledge and technology into the curriculum, maintain and develop local culture, teach respect, commitment, responsibility, self-reliance, skills for life and survival, and training in the home location.

Interview with Malon William and Tom Wass

In February 2002, I spoke with Malon William, the president of Bowie Church Youth, and Tom Wass, both from Hog Harbour village, east of Santo. Both share the following views:

• We think that the question of the decline of youth membership is a very good question. The church needs to find out why this is so and then solve the matter before our entire youth move to other sects or stay at home and become like lost sheep without a shepherd. According to their own Constitution it is the church's responsibility to do something (*Presbyterian Church Vanuatu Constitution*, p. 12, 5:2.6, under the heading 'Building up the Christian and Witness').

- During the period of their youth, people develop both in body and mind, so at this stage youth will want to explore new things. Therefore the church needs to think about this because there are so many things to explore in our society today. But the church has to teach the youth and show them what is right in order to prepare them as future leaders of our church, society and nation. In our presbytery we see that the youth have been ignored by their local Sessions. We see that all the programs that should be carried out have not been carried out because the parents are not Christians, but are backsliders, and not interested in church activities, so they do not encourage their children to participate.
- Another issue is the way in which God's message is taught and preached. Many preachers do not actually preach from the Bible texts but make up their own points focusing on people's weaknesses. We think that what should be first is the Bible message, then its application to life. We also think that the it is very difficult to communicate between the various youth groups within our presbytery, so it is hard for the youth in each local Session to encourage and help strengthen other youth groups, so this in turn creates a youth decline.
- The problem can only be solved if the church takes action quickly. It needs to work more closely with youth in the congregations, especially in the rural areas. This means that the church needs to see that the youth activities suit their interests, and involve youth in church activities such as choir singing, reading, prayer, leading worship – that is, delegating responsibilities to youth during big events of church and society. Also if the youth have their own pastor at the Presbytery level, then this will help; Efate Presbytery has done it and it has helped them a lot.

Conclusion

I would like to conclude by expressing the hope that this paper will be helpful in pointing out the reasons for the decline of youth membership in the Presbyterian Church of Vanuatu, and also will help us to find solutions, in order to prepare the youth for their future responsibilities as leaders of church, society and nation. Perhaps this will also be helpful to other churches that have the same problem.

Social Development in Vanuatu:
A Challenge to the Churches

William Bice Qorig

Introduction

Urban growth has had a similar socio-economic impact in Vanuatu as it has in other Pacific Island nations, particularly in the Melanesian group. For instance, in the two most urbanised areas of the country, namely Port Vila and Luganville, there is inadequate housing for the low and middle income groups, lack of proper sanitation, and inadequate provision of services such as water, electricity, transport facilities and many other amenities. This has led to the creation of a well-known expression to most ni-Vanuatu: SPR or *sperem pablik rod*. The term meaning 'unemployed' reflects the current economic crisis in the country. Whether it is 'Mr. Liu' in the Solomon Islands or similar phrases in PNG, it refers to the problems caused by unemployment.

This paper contemplates some issues that are in most cases the result of urbanization. There are other socio-economic problems involved and there a lot of issues that many social planners, economists and other experts may identify. Therefore this paper will seek to help the reader to understand the context of SPR and evaluate it from biblical perspectives. It will also help the reader to know what other people's views are on this subject. Finally it will provide some possibilities, choices and alternatives that may help in dealing with this issue. This paper is not a solution to be followed, but a road map to help see the problem in our time.

Concept of social development in the local cultures

Whether we live in a traditional community, with communities that have undergone wider change in recent years, or with some other kinds of communities that are forming in Melanesia, a close look at traditional communities will help us appreciate how people understand and think about their relationship with each other. According to Pastor Kalsakau Urtalo's lectures, a local community could simply mean, 'a group of people who come from the same area, speaking the same language'. Their main characteristics may be common kinship, common language, common place or area of origin, common social or religious association, and especially common beliefs in the principle of mutual reciprocity.[98]

Home and family

Traditionally in our culture, life in the community was a life of strong relationship within family lines and tribes. Every man, woman and child lived as a group-oriented and not individualistic person. In every activity of life people needed each other's support, without which no-one could survive. This culture is built into their life and has affected the way they do their barter system, exchanging of foods, and helping when a family need arises such as bride-price, compensation, sickness, death etc. In one way or the other culture plays a very important part in binding and strengthening the people, and their traditions impact on their ways of life and their relationships.[99]

Parents work together to provide for the physical, spiritual and emotional well-being of their family. They never expect any one else to take care of this responsibility. Children do their part in the work of the family, doing the work assignments that best fit their abilities. Sometimes people encounter hardships when trying to provide for their families but if we are in this situation we must continue to be faithful in carrying out our duties. To some people work is drudgery but to others it is an exciting part of life. One way to enjoy life to its fullest is to learn to love work. The life of the family, tribes, or society as a whole can mean a life of unity where common understanding is strong.

2. Community norms

Every community in Vanuatu has a chief, sometimes more than one. The work of the chief in the community is to maintain peace and unity among the people, to solve the problems and differences that might arise, to protect and preserve our culture and to make sure people live in peace and harmony with one another and their neighbours. All people of Vanuatu must cultivate and treasure the sense of common purpose and a desire for common destiny.[100] This is the reason why the ideas about peace must be updated. We want to hold the country together because we believe in the universal values of democracy as guidelines for building justice in human societies.[101]

The Malvatumauri Council of Chiefs is a national organization comprising all chiefs from each island of our six provinces. These chiefs are chosen to represent their people in the Council of Chiefs. Here is the status and structure of how the Malvatumauri functions from village level upwards:

[Insert Image]

a. The Malvatumauri is mandated by the Government on Customary matters. Before any bill concerning custom land, etc., goes before the Parliament, consultation must be held with the National Council of Chiefs.[102]
b. The Malvatumauri is mandated to protect, promote and teach custom, culture, tradition and language in the country.[103]
c. The Malvatumauri is mandated to protect the integrity of our custom chiefs through recognition, respect and honour.[104]

As responsible leaders we should see that unity and peace, respect and honour are maintained at all times from the village level up to the national level. As leaders we must also prioritise to improve villages, develop individual provinces, improve provincial government and make sure the central government has consistent consultation with provincial government in matters of governance and development.

The key aspect of development to address now is that of the health of the national economy. This is obvious for without it there will be no social services and the government cannot render effectively its services to the public. The village chiefs must continue to assert their influence and authority in their own communities. They should not only arbitrate between disputing parties, but play a greater role in managing and leading their village people.

3. Land tenures

All members of the community have access to the resources of the area according to the norms established over generations. Land as the basis of subsistence agriculture is one of the most important resources in Vanuatu. It is the heart of the operation of the cultural system, thus representing life, materially and spiritually. However, each person must have a place, some land to control, since if he does not have any land, he has no roots, status or power. In the most extreme case this means he is denied social existence.[105]

Colonization has overturned the old structure of the distribution of land, thus creating what is known today as customary land disputes. Land disputes were almost unknown traditionally but since Christianity came and brought the people together (even the mountain people came to live in groups near the shore), the land tenure system has been disrupted.[106] Some areas were over-populated and new methods of production were introduced and the old relationship between man and the soil was changed. In the most extreme cases, land hunger, which did not exist in traditional society, began to be felt and the relationship between man and the soil, which was first mystical and cultural, become economic.

In Vanuatu society today there is a movement towards the purchase and sale of land particularly when people are moving from over-populated to under-populated areas. The Vanuatu Constitution allowed special provision to be made for urban land, thus allowing the government to declare that some customary land would become public. In this case, it does not mean that the land is owned by the Government or any statutory bodies set up for the purpose, but it would be managed by them. Customary owners would be involved in the management and share part of any revenue raised. It was to be rather like a compulsory lease, with the amount of rent to customary owners being dependent on revenue collected.[107]

Connection with land remains certainly one of the deepest values of our culture and it also marks the country's unique cultural identity.

Social development in the post-Independence era

Modernization and civilisation have greatly increased the rate of social and cultural change, bringing a bewildering farrago of new values, attitudes, ideas, conventions, impressions, images and symbols, other interpretations of reality and the universe, new technology, doctrines and dogmas, and in many cases destroying our traditional cultures. Many people have moved from their village settlements to an urban settlement. The Second World War saw the true beginning of urban development in Vanuatu and the rapid introduction of urban infrastructure in Port Vila on Efate and also in Luganville on Santo.[108] The war brought thousands of ni-Vanuatu into contact with urban life for the first time.[109]

Our national views of the urban trend have become ambivalent, reflecting our different experiences of the outcome of the urban processes. My intention in this paper is to describe some of those ways that the story is told from various disciplines, before returning to my own theological perspective upon SPR.

1. Population growth

At the time of the 1989 census, the population of Vanuatu was 142,149. The annual population growth rate was 2.9 percent for the next ten years to the 1999 census, when the population increased to 186,678. In this latter census, in Port Vila the population was 29,356 and in Luganville 10,738. Rapid urbanization in Vanuatu is primarily due to high rates of population mobility. Migration appears to be changing from the traditional rural based circular movement to more permanent rural urban flows.[110]

Cities attract people from rural areas because cities promise a better quality of life, better employment opportunities, better educational and health facilities. They promise for many the possibility of sheer survival. Additionally, in today's modern culture, as more of the country's population live in Port Vila and Luganville, one does not even have to live in the city in order to be saturated by its values, style and urban imagery. This overlay of local or rural cultures by urban modes of thinking and acting is termed 'urbanism' and is so powerfully infectious that it is sometimes difficult for those thus influenced even to be aware that it is happening to them.[111]

It is a challenge for the people and the Government of Vanuatu to take the necessary steps in choosing their future. There is time to act while the population is small, and education and health systems are in place, although improvements in these services are needed. Recognition of the challenges which the rapid population growth presents points to the urgent need for improved economic conditions.[112]

2. Education better and more

The 1999 census estimates were that 55.8 percent of Vanuatu's economically active population had only primary education or no education at all, and 16.8 percent had secondary school education up to year 10. Formal education is low even among the highest-level occupations where about half have only primary education. The information shows that Vanuatu is failing to educate all its young today and the enrolment rate seems very low. The reality is that Vanuatu, which already has an education system that is extremely costly will not be able to offer the basic 10 years of schooling to all children without directing substantially more resources to education.[113] But it is improved education that will increase the skill levels of Vanuatu's workforce and reduce unemployment in Vanuatu.

Impact of SPR in urban areas

Crime and other forms of deviant behaviour such as prostitution, vagrancy, alcohol abuse and breaking up of families have been singled out as the most pressing problems in the country today. The observation that such behaviour occurs more frequently in cities than in rural areas has prompted numerous sociological explanations. It is believed that the rapid urbanization and migration from rural areas results in the breaking down of traditional and social control. Migrants who come to the city lose their cultural identity and join the urban population, and it is likely to be responsible for crime, matrimonial disharmony, child neglect, prostitution and so on. The consequences are unemployment or SPR. People likely to be involved are those ranging in age from 15 to 30, mostly school leavers without jobs.

Case studies

Here are some examples of the sort of problems we find arising today.

They are drawn from real life experience but all individuals described have been given fictitious names.

Example 1: James and Jenny have not married because Jenny was going to have a baby. They first met two years earlier. They went to see the pastor; they hoped to get married later on. Both were secondary school leavers without jobs. Some time after, they went to Port Vila seeking to find a job and live for the time being with James' brother who works in one of the restaurants in town. As the weeks went by, James did not find a job; he spent most of his time strolling the streets, finding his school mates, drinking kava and alcohol and sometimes winding up in night clubs. He ended up going home late at nights, thus creating a lot of quarrels between him and Jenny. James seems to have had a number of adventures with other women. For several weeks, his wife knew nothing of this, but when she did find out, James decided to divorce her, leaving her alone with their eight-months-old baby.

Example 2: Because there are great problems of poverty today and not enough work for educated people in villages, many girls refuse to stay with their parents at home. They decide to leave and go to the towns. What happens is that they become prostitutes in order to gain money for themselves to survive in the town. One student from a Secondary School I met some years ago told me that her parents were no longer paying for her school fees and she was responsible for her own fees.

Example 3: Late one evening, some members of Mango Station called me to intervene in a noisy fight between two different groups in Luganville Town. I came to where the people were arguing and fighting. I could sense that things were serious, because they were talking very heatedly. I could see the two angry crowds of people carrying on with their exchange of insulting words and I could hear people whispering to their friends 'Hush, police, police'. Gradually the problem become clear; a man in one group married a woman whose father had belonged to another group. During the husband's absence from home, his own father had said insulting words to the woman, his daughter-in-law, and had made immoral suggestions to her. This created ill feeling between the two family groups. Realizing the problem, the chiefs settled the problem but those found guilty were arrested by the police and were taken into prison.

Too often, the natural desire is that many young people today who are unemployed and are SPR can cause a lot of problems. As mentioned above, deviant forms of behaviour such as stealing, fighting, rape and many others are consequences of unemployment or SPR. Many marriages fail because people get married without considering or understanding what this new relationship will mean for their lives. They are quite unprepared and unfortunately break up.

This does not mean that all Christian marriages will always show stability. Because we are sinful, Christians also often fail in their marriages and in their family life. But within the family, in the relationship between husband and wife and the relationship between parents and children, what is important is to reflect the love of God, the act of sharing and compassion, respect and care. In order to maintain a good marriage situation and change deviant or criminal behaviour, all we need is repentance and forgiveness.

In an Introduction to Crime Prevention, Sergeant Titus Taripu in the Crime Prevention Office highlighted a few important points when he said:

> *Blong gat gudfala Crime Prevention, man mo woman, yumi mas gat strong bilif or tingting long fasin blong stopem ol trabol ikam antap. Mo blong talem tu se, Crime Prevention hemi no wok blong polis nomo, be polis mo Pablik tugeta. Hemia I minim se yumi evri citizen i mas wok tugeta blong daonem ol fasin nogud long kantri blong yumi. Mo oltaem yumi mas kipim Vanuatu blong yumi hemi wan prapa ples blong stap long hem oltaem.*

In order for there to be good crime prevention, both men and women must think seriously about crime so that it doesn't increase. Furthermore, crime prevention is not the work only of the police, but of the police and the public together. This means that every citizen must cooperate together in decreasing bad behaviour in our nation. We must maintain our nation of Vanuatu as a good place to be.

As long as we live, our development and growth have not finished. We are still 'becoming'.[114] This means we can look back to the way we lived our lives in the past, and be free, and we can look forward to the future towards which we are moving. Our past life influences us, but it need not hold us a prisoner. As we grow, we can change direction, like a plant that turns towards the light.[115] Jesus sees possibilities of growth and development in the life of every person. Growth in knowledge and character is possible when a person becomes united in Christ (2 Peter 3:18).

The Christian in the urban area

Every Christian is part of the wider family of God's household, the church (1 Timothy 3:15, Ephesians 2:19). It is true, however, that urban areas provide new possibilities of interchange between people; they bring people together into a common narrative, but their stories are nevertheless specific and different. We must learn to discern what is going on around us and not to depart from the Christian mores and values based upon the traditions of our faith; as the Quaker Communities express it, we must engage not in the war of the beast, but in the war of the lamb.

1. Understanding people

In any sort of work we need to know and understand who or what it is we are working with. For most forms of ministry some understanding of people is necessary. For a Christian this is especially important because people and their thoughts, feelings, doubts and fears, their hopes and joys are the chief concern. And so it is important, for the ministry of pastoral care especially, that we understand people and their needs. Pastoral care depends on the Christian's ability to work with people, so we need to know people, and understand the life they lead if we are going to help them in any effective way. We need to develop the skills of good personal relationships. How we deal with people and treat them depends on what we believe about them. If we believe that people are of great worth, then we will show this in the way we treat them. So it is important that we should practice the commandment of God 'to love'. Mark 12:23 says that we must love one another as we love ourselves. Sometimes we treat people in a way that shows we do not think very highly of them. If someone asks us what a particular person is like, we usually describe them in ways that reflect our own opinion of them or relationship with them. We say, 'she is a pretty girl', or, 'she is a prostitute,' or, 'he is a vagrant, unemployed or an "SPR"'. While there are many different ways of describing people, it is important for us to understand them in the light of God's Word (Galatians 5:22–23), which concentrates on the fruits of the spirit.

In this light, SPR is a wrong concept to use in the church. When we say people are SPR, it's like saying that God made a mistake in creating people. But I believe that God created all people to do good works and to serve God, whether or not they are paid money for what they do. The Christian view of human beings is to understand people based upon the foundation of God's revelation of his purpose for all mankind in the world based on the Bible.

2. The biblical view

The creation narrative in the book of Genesis gives us an understanding of humans as being created in the image of God (Genesis 1:26–28). These verses have been explained in many different ways, but whatever we might say, humanity has been created to have a very special place in God's creation. That is, we are more special than the other creatures God created and our brains are more highly developed. In this case we are able to think and to reason. Because we are able to think and to be in fellowship with

God, God gave us the responsibility of controlling his creation and using it according to his purpose.

Our lives can be separated from God as described in Genesis 3:7–19. Adam and Eve were shut out of the garden because of sin. For this reason, it does not mean that God after putting the humans out of the garden took all the responsibilities away from them in controlling his creation. It is to say that God, having created the whole creation, is creating work for humans. Because of this reason he said to the man 'You have to sweat to work'. In the New Testament in the teachings of Jesus, he uses parables to show that a good servant must be a good workman. In the parable of the labourers in the vineyard (Matthew 20:1–16), we note the following points: that a man has a right to work, that a man has a right to a living wage, that a man has a right to reasonable working conditions.

Paul in 1 Corinthians 4:12 says that we must work hard with our own hands. Paul even emphasises that we are God's workmanship, created in Christ Jesus to do good works (Ephesians 2:10). Paul also said 'If a man will not work, then let him not eat' (2 Thessalonians 3:10). Not everybody will find work for pay in the towns of Port Vila and Luganville. Therefore we should not talk about unemployment or SPR but we should talk about the reality that we are created in God's image and we are created to do good works.

3. The church (the body of Christ)

If Jesus, Son of God, is the light of the world, then the church is the light to the world. Jesus is the light of the world and the head of the church, and we are the members with divine responsibilities to shine out or to introduce that light into the dark areas of human conduct. (Matthew 5:14). The church as the body of Christ is the community of people called and chosen to live holy lives (1 Peter 1:15–16). All Christians are to obey and follow the ways of God and walk in them (Deuteronomy 10:12). The church should then adopt Jesus' direct strategy of being alongside the poor, with those in need, and always asking who is most benefiting from our actions: ourselves or God's poor through whom he saves the world. Our question now must be: Is the church up-to-speed in the situation? or What is the Mission of God in this urbanizing world, and how can the church as the body of Christ deal with this situation?

Our urban mission must be a mission that is open for all people of good will – a mission for the poor, the needy or the SPRs. The operation of a holy church in today's urban setting will often be a mission that needs to learn the disciplines and prepare ourselves, researching prayerfully and reflecting theologically before making any assumption about what might be God's Good News to this situation. We must listen, watch and act with solidarity.[116] We can make the same point using other words of the New Testament, 'For our fight is not against flesh and blood but against the powers and principalities of this dark age' (Ephesians 6:12).

Theological reflection

As Creator, God is responsible for creating human beings in his own image; human beings were created to be sons and daughters of God who by the work of the Spirit, enables them to be in relationship with him, calling him 'Father' (Romans 8:15–17). God the creator or Father has also placed humans in a created world as an arena for personal creativity, social cooperation and harmony.[117] As part of the creation mandate given to humanity, we are to care for nature as God's stewards.

The Bible says 'For God so loved the world that he gave his only Son, that whoever believes in Him should not perish, but have everlasting life' (John 3:16) – an unconditional love for sinners! What did God see? What state were we in that God should die for us? He saved us when we were yet in sin; he rescued us from being lost forever. If God died, a righteous person for us sinners, then I believe we have an obligation to extend, or share love with the so-called SPR. We should see them with the eyes of concern, love and compassion. God saw us that way and He came as one of us, and died for us. He became one of us, dwelt and ate with us. The SPR are lost, therefore as Christians, a pastor or church members, we should go to these people to help them. We should take every opportunity that arises to reach out to them with the Word of God. Jesus suffered to save us; therefore for us, there is likely to be suffering and persecution too. But as Christians we remember that our Lord went through this, so we can do it for Christ's sake.

Therefore my position is that not everybody will find work for payment in the two towns, Port Vila and Luganville. In our ethics of work in Vanuatu, we should not talk about 'unemployment' but talk about the importance and the reality that we are all created in God's image, and we are created to do good works. People in general have the capacity to think and work. Therefore, we ni-Vanuatu should encourage all aspects of work; that is so whether we work for pay or provide our own daily living by gardening or fishing; to sustain life is very important. We should do all we can to assist others in daily living. Our forefathers survived without money for many years, just on gardening, fishing, hunting and sharing. In a context of a cash economy where the majority of our people live in the islands, we should encourage subsistence farming and train our people to use their own hands, rather than look elsewhere to provide work. Unemployment is a wrong concept to use in the church. When we say people are unemployed, it is like saying God made a mistake in creating people, or he created people like robots, which can only perform their duty when the right batteries are put in and the right buttons are pressed. I believe that God created all people to do good work, whether or not they are paid money or contribute to their daily survival to serve God.

1. Views of other people

An arrangement was made to interview some staff and students from Talua Ministry Training Centre. The response supports what has been written in this paper. As a result of these interviews, this next part is divided into two different sections (a) the positives and (b) the negatives.

a. The positives

The positive view is that we can no longer call SPRs 'Sperem Public Rod', but rather we ought to call them 'Special Productive Resources'. The Government and the church should take initiatives to design training courses in order to help such people, in particular young people, to be productive in their lives. If we engage them in training, it will help them to get jobs and be able to earn their own living. Further, Rural Training Centres around the country were set up for this purpose, so that young people can obtain certain skills to help them to be useful to their own communities.

It was also agreed that we should pray for them. We are to make meaningful contact with these people who are lost and are not yet Christians, build significant personal relationships and friendship with them. We must create an environment where the Good News can be introduced informally and naturally, maybe through creative activities.

b. The negatives

The negative view was that the so-called SPRs are economically handicapped. Some people may be physically ill or handicapped and unable to work. Some may not have the skills to get a decent job. They agreed that we must avoid giving 'hand outs' (free food, clothing. Etc.) but try to find ways in which they can work to earn the things that are their immediate needs. In return for work, they can be given some food or clothing, etc, but not money. If they will not work, and do not want to change their way of life or hear the Gospel Message, then they should be told that we cannot help them. It was also agreed that if the SPRs continue to display behaviour that is bad, they should be given corporal punishment.

2. Possibilities and alternatives

As there are many ways people can become poor, so there are different ways of dealing with each case. There are no simple solutions. Each situation must be examined. Some cases will involve more than one factor. There is no best solution but only suggestions. One has to see the following alternatives as a guide and not the only way:

- God's church must be prepared to welcome and accept anyone, just as God accepts us.
- We must tell SPRs of God's love, and that any assistance we give is given in the Name of the Lord Jesus Christ.
- The best way to help such people is to provide them with ways to help themselves.
- Families should take care of their own.
- In the light of the Word of God, the church should welcome those involved and use scriptural understanding as their guidelines.
- The pastor and the church should see SPRs as an opportunity to preach the gospel. If they need food, give them a job helping to harvest copra or something like that, and if they cannot work, look for their family to see if they can help them.

Conclusion: The moral decision

Sperem Public Rod is a wrong concept to use in the church. Rather we should be saying that these people are created in the image of God. They can be called 'Special Potential Resources'. They are people of Vanuatu, having the blood of Vanuatu in them, so therefore we must not neglect them. We must also realise that in Vanuatu even though he or she is an SPR, he or she is still ni-Vanuatu.

Furthermore, it is our responsibility to serve others, for Jesus said, 'It is not the healthy who need a doctor, but the sick' (Matthew 9:12). Service is helping others who need assistance. Christ-like service grows out of genuine love for the Saviour and of love and concern for those whom he gives as opportunities and directions to help. Love is more than a feeling; when we love others, we want to help them.

Bibliography

Connell, John, & John, P Leo, *Pacific 2010: Planning the future Melanesian Cities in 2010*, Sydney: National Centre for Development Studies, 1993

Green, Laurie, *The Impact of the Global: An Urban Theology*, Place: Benfoy Press, 2001

Hardiman, Margaret, Midgley James (ed), *The Social Dimensions of Development: Social Policy and Planning in the Third World* London School of Economics & Political Science, John Wiley & Sons Limited, 1982

Larmour, Peter, *Land Tenure in Vanuatu*, Suva: University of the South Pacific, 1984

Tait, Maree, *Pacific 2010: Strategies for Vanuatu*, Sydney: National Centre for Development Studies, 1994

Taylor, Harold, *Tend My Sheep*, London: SPCK, 1983

Titus, Sergeant Taripu, *Holem Han Tugeta*, Port Vila: Vanuatu Police Department: Crime Prevention Section

Wilson, Brother Tarimure Cliff, *The Role of the Solomon Islands Christian Association (SICA) and The Melanesian Brotherhood (MBH) in the Ethnic Tension before the Townsville Peace Agreement*, Kohimarama, Honiara, 2002

Interviews

Pastor Kalsakau Urtalo, Lecturer, Pacific Culture, Talua Ministry Training Centre, 2002

Ismael Sandy, Secretary, Malvatumauri Council of Chief, Port Vila, personal interview, 2003

Conclusion

There is a lot of energy among the churches in Vanuatu for tackling the issues of the relationship between the Christian gospel and the cultures of Vanuatu.

The fact that such a large quantity of material was submitted for this publication, leading to a requirement to produce two separate books, is an indication of this. More importantly, there seems to be an emerging confidence on the part of local church people to speak their mind on gospel and culture issues and to put their ideas into print. As noted in the conclusion to the previous volume: 'There are indications that the younger generation of leaders are able to explore the issues of gospel and culture in an open way, neither blindly accepting the traditional approach of the early missionaries nor rejecting their approach out of hand. There is a readiness to respect their own cultures while exploring how the Christian gospel engages with these cultures.'

A further observation in the conclusion to the previous volume is also worthy of repetition:

> There is also a basic issue about the authority of the Scriptures as a resource for dealing with various particular themes of gospel and culture. The churches in the South Pacific have inherited the nineteenth-century missionary views of the Bible as the authoritative voice of God on all matters, which means that the Bible is often used in the form of proof texts. On the other hand there are numbers of local people who are increasingly influenced by more recent scholarship about the origin and the purpose of the Scriptures, and are not so ready to accept the literal authority of the Bible. What the Bible is, how we are to read and interpret it, and how it addresses particular themes of gospel and culture, remains a big issue for the Vanuatu church.

This series of volumes is also serving the purpose of gathering together unique historical and cultural material, and providing an avenue where new research can be documented and preserved. This will prove to be a valuable resource in the future. In this volume the Church of Melanesia material about the Banks Islands and the article about the Protestant Church of Vanuatu are good examples.

Where to now? As noted already, this volume (with a twin volume of similar material to be produced within a few months) breaks new ground. The local people are increasingly responsible for its authorship and for the process of gathering the material to be published.

This volume is also considerably more ecumenical in its breadth than the previous three volumes, with contributions from the Church of Melanesia, which is now a partner in the Talua Ministry Training Centre, the Evangelical Protestant Church, and the Catholic Church. It is hoped that this ecumenical involvement will grow, providing opportunities for varying perspectives on church history, varying local experiences of church life, and varying approaches to the way in which the gospel engages with local cultures to be articulated. All church traditions in Vanuatu are confronted by the same challenges and it would be a real benefit if there can be more conversation across the churches about how to respond.

There has been informal discussion about two other ideas that would lead to further publications in this series. This year, 2005, marks the silver jubilee of Vanuatu's independence. It has been suggested that there might be a volume that marks this anniversary and considers how issues of gospel and culture have been tackled in the twenty-five-year history of Vanuatu. Secondly, discussion has continued about the value of having a good reference book on gospel and culture for use at the local ministry training centre. This too would constitute a very worthwhile development.

Randall Prior

Endnotes

1 Prior 1998, p. 77. Here he holds that *tam-tam* is a totem symbol but it may not symbolise any animal or plant.

2 The three elements of the *tam-tam* are based on the oral witness of Philip Joses, a student of Talua Ministry Training Centre. According to him, different tribes are classified by the number of faces in the *tam-tam*, one face to five faces. A pig or even money is used to change one's social status from a fewer-numbered-face tribe to a more-numbered-face tribe. The club for pig-killing is usually leaned against the *tam-tam* vertically, not horizontally as we see in Loughman's picture.

3 All stories in this section were collected by Colin Steve Sosori, a student of Talua MTC and added to by Viralivliv (Ruben Todali), who is called the Professor of Cultural Stories in Pentecost Island. Sosori and I visited professor Viralivliv on 21 September 2002, guided by Father Stanley Ure.

4 Vanuatu, also known as the New Hebrides, was under the joint administration of an Anglo-French Condominium from 1906 until its independence in 1980. An idea of this impact can be gauged from the guidebook written by O'Byrne and Harcombe, and the book by Tippett (see bibliography for complete details of these and other references given in these footnotes).

5 In 2003, the illiteracy rate was close to 54 percent, with primary school dropouts a common occurrence even in the capital Port Vila. This was due primarily to a lack of financial and human resources for the primary school students and the teachers. The average annual income per capita was equivalent to AUD3,000.00 or Vatu 250,000. The average age of the population is 16 years of age and the average life span is in the mid-40s!

6 Quoting an article on an extract from George Soros' *The Bubble of American Supremacy* (Sydney: Allen & Unwin, 2004), in the Sydney Morning Herald, 'Globalisation – Lopsided Generator of Wealth', 2 February 2004.

7 Over the past twenty years, Western cults like the Jehovah Witnesses, the Mormons and the Baha'i are posing an increasing threat to the integrity of the gospel via their socio-economic and education programs to a nation impoverished through globalisation. See Prior 2003, p. 182.

8 Prior 1999.

9 Prior 2003, p. 187.

10 Hillard. In the rural regions where there are churches, village life was centred around the Christian worship, with dawn and sometimes evening devotions as well. A personal experience in the island of Nguna in the Efate Presbytery in April–May 2004.

11 A survey of their understanding of the gospel was noted in a recent survey by the Vanuatu Council of Churches in Santo, Vanuatu where an average of 58 representatives and church leaders gave their views on their understanding of the gospel (Prior 1995). Although this does not represent all the Christians in Vanuatu, this constitutes more than 90 percent of the Christian population, as most of them belong to the Presbyterian denomination.

12 A personal observation as a lecturer at Talua Ministry Training Centre in September–November 2004 (and with the added advantage of interviewing the students and staff directly on the topic).

13 A tract written by a son of the indigenous pastor Jack Loughman was a case in point. Prior 1998, pp. 66–85.

14 Examples of the latter would be the Roman Catholics and the Seven Day Adventists. They prescribe to the Apostolic Creed.

15 This contractual agreement is upheld to the present day. The Anglican Church of Vanuatu is the forerunner of the Church of Melanesia.

16 The Cargo Cult was led by a retired US Army soldier from World War II in early 1942. John Frum, the cult leader, set up the cult in Tanna, a southern island of Vanuatu. There is still a residual but dwindling group of followers on this island and they are generally regarded as a relic from the past. The name Cargo is due to the cult leader's promise that he would return with cargoes of free goods for his followers.

17 Before the coming of missionaries in the mid-19th century, the primary mode of their history and traditions are passed on from generations to generations via oral traditions only. There were not many available written records other than those from the pioneer missionaries' diaries. Miller, *Live* Vol. 2.

18 Miller, Vol. 2., p. 146.

19 See J. Naual, 'Examining the Concept an Nature of Conversion in the Presbyterian Church of Vanuatu in Contrast to Biblical Conversion', in Prior 2003, pp. 175–188.

20 Prior 1995.

21 Naual in Prior 2003, p. 182.

22 Ibid., p. 183.

23 Most of these issues are dealt with in Prior 2003.

24 Prior 2001, pp. 147–9.

25 See Tanihi.

26 As Vanuatu comprises of 83 islands with a diversity of languages, traditions and customs, we can only take a more generalised view of their understanding of the gospel from literature currently available.

27 Through their socio-economic and education programs, the Mormons, Ba'hai and Jehovah Witnesses are making their presence in Vanuatu felt since the early 1990s. Islam was introduced to the island of Tanna in the south in the early 1990s, but does not seem to have a strong following amongst the locals. The Australian Presbyterian World Mission and Chinese Christian Mission Australia are examples evangelical groups that have responded.

28 I have deliberately excluded the Roman Catholic Church's activities, as their sacramentalism in goals and direction in the interpretation of the Great Commission is at odds with the biblical revelation. An example of this can be seen in the article by Talal Asad, 'Comments on Conversion', in Van Der Veer, pp. 263–72. Also the article written by Margaret Jolly on the Roman Catholics' intention and goals, 'Devils, Holy Spirits, and the Swollen God: Translation, Conversion and Colonial Power in the Marist Mission, Vanuatu, 1887–1934', in Van Der Veer, pp. 231–62.

29 A case in point would be John Williams, who was martyred soon after his arrival on the

island of Erromanga in November 1839.

30 For examples of John Geddie's experience of the natives' customs and cannibalism in Aneityum, a southern island of New Hebrides in 1850–1856, see Prior 1998, pp. 17-21.

31 Widow-strangling was a popular local custom in Geddie's time in the 1840s. On the death of her husband, the widow would be strangled so that she could continue to serve the deceased in the heathen world as a sign of faithfulness to him. Prior 1998, p. 12.

32 Prior's impression of Geddie's Missionary Strategy. Prior 1998, p. 54.

33 Prior's conclusion to his understanding of the primary documents written by Geddie, 2 January 1851 to 3 October 1854. Prior 1998, p. 38.

34 For example, through a contractual agreement in the early-nineteenth century to share the load of evangelism, the Anglicans under Bishop Selwyn and the Presbyterians under Geddie agreed 'to carve out' their mission field whereby the Anglicans (latter known as the Church of Melanesia) have prime pastoral and evangelistic concern of the islands in the North and the Presbyterians of the islands in the South. This contractual agreement is still being honoured.

35 Huntington postulated this clash would be the result of irreconcilable differences in the age of globalisation between rich and poor nations on socio-economic, political and cultural differences (as the richer nations and multinational organisations would exploit the poorer ones and become richer and the poor becomes poorer). Huntington, pp. 22 25, 67.

36 A good summary of this can be found in the article by Chee Pang Choong in Hutchinson, pp. 214–26.

37 Section 3, Chapter 11, 'Religion and the Future of Christianity', in Tiplady, *One World or Many*.

38 Hutchinson, *Global Faith*, pp. 5–25.

39 Vanuatu, formerly known as the New Hebrides, was a joint Anglo-French Condominium since 1906. Its independence in July 1980 coincided approximately with the rising influence of globalisation.

40 It is to be noted that even within the 83 islands of Vanuatu, there exist heterogeneous diversities in their traditions, religion and even languages. But these differences are of a relative and minor nature in comparison. Perspectives on these differences can be found in Part 1 of Prior 2003, pp. 1–121.

41 Prior 2003, p. 133. There are four chiefs directly under his command and for each of the four, there are eighteen other subordinate chiefs, each with their own *nakamal* (chief's meeting house) in the island of Makira.

42 See Naual's article, 'Examining the Concept and Nature of Conversion in the Presbyterian Church of Vanuatu in Contrast to Biblical Conversion', in Prior 2003, pp. 182–3.

43 Chief Will Bongmatur, Chief Noel Mariesua, the first President Ati George Sokomanu and the first Prime Minister Father Walter Lini are Christians and instrumental in the planning and implementation of the independence of Vanuatu from the Anglo-French Condominium based upon a Christian style of Constitution. Prior 2001, p. 26.

44 On a recent Sunday service at Serate Presbyterian Church (10

September 2004), a village in the northern island of Santo, Vanuatu, I, as an ordained Presbyterian Minister of Australia, needed to obtain permission from the village chief before entering the village to conduct the service. It is worth noting that the chief himself is an elder of the church. This permission procedure is still vigorously enforced.

45 Robertson, pp. 264-81. He is generally seen as the father of the Pittsburgh School in the sociology of religion, as he formulated a 'globalisation paradigm' on what the impact globalisation would has upon a nation's culture and religious beliefs.

46 Quoting W. R. Garrett, p. 301.

47 K. Z. Urtalo, 'Pig-Killing as a means of providing a good life', in Prior 2001, pp. 42-8.

48 A conclusion from Ambrym Presbytery on the topic of 'Marriage and in Santo-Malo Presbytery', in Prior 2003, pp. 75-80, 115-20.

49 Quoting D. M. Lewis, 'Globalization: The Problem of Definition and Future Areas of Historical Inquiry', in Hutchinson, *Global Faith*, p. 33.

50 Stackhouse, *Global Future*, p. 109.

51 Quoting Lewis, 'Globalization', in Hutchinson, *Global Faith*, pp. 39-40.

52 The forerunner of the Church of Melanesia is the Vanuatu Anglican Church.

53 The Vanuatu Council of Churches consists of the Presbyterian Church of Vanuatu, the Church of Melanesia, the Church of Christ, the Apostolic Church of Vanuatu and the Roman Catholics, with the Assembly of God and the Seventh Day Adventist as observers only.

54 Prior 2003,pp. 182-3.

55 Richard Osmer nicely summarises using these three terms in 'The Teaching Ministry in a Multi-cultural World', in Stackhouse, *God and Globalization*, Vol. 2, pp. 55-75.

56 Chinese Christian Mission Australia organised twelve short-term missions to Melanesia and remote parts of Australia and New Zealand in 2004, and it is envisaged that fifteen short-term missions will be made in 2005.

57 Examples of these are the Jehovah Witnesses, the Mormons or Latter Day Saints, and the Ba'hai, just to mention a few that are active in Vanuatu. The extent of their involvement differs between the islands.

58 Quoting an article on an extract from George Soros' book *The Bubble of American Supremacy* (Sydney: Allen & Unwin, 2004), in the Sydney Morning Herald, 'Globalisation – Lopsided Generator of Wealth', 2 February 2004.

59 As noted in the General Assembly of the Presbyterian Church of Vanuatu that took place in Malakula, September 2004.

60 Interview with Mr. Lancolit Wotlemaro, 9 March 2002.

61 Interview with Fred Sagler.

62 Ibid.

63 Interview with Fred Sagler, 16 April 2002.

64 Ibid.

65 Interview with Fred Sagler, 09 May 2002.

66 Interview with Fr. Ezekeil Tias, 04 June 2002.

67 Miller, *Live* Book 3, p. 12

68 Fox, p. 133.

69 Ibid., p. 125.

70 Ibid., p. 5.

71 Miller, *Live* Book 1, p. 145.

72 Interview with Fr. Ezekiel Tias, 04 June 2002.

73 Ibid.

74 Ibid.

75 Ibid.

76 Ibid.

77 Ibid.

78 Ibid.

79 Ibid.

80 Ibid.

81 Stanley W. Womack & Jones L.Tognse, *They Came to My Island* (by George Sarawin), Port Vila: Pars Printing, 1996, p. 2.

82 Fox, p. 135.

83 Ibid., p. 135.

84 Ibid, p. 126.

85 Interview with Fr. John Benneth, 11 July 2002.

86 Ibid.

87 Fox, p. 134.

88 Ibid., p. 135.

89 Ibid., p. 40.

90 Ibid., pp. 141–2

91 Ibid., p. 104.

92 Interview with Elder Johnny Albert at Rovo Bay, EPI, 30 October 2002.

93 Interview with Youth Desk President, Richard Tadwin, at Magam, Ambrym, 29 June 2002.

94 Interview with Dr. Titus Path at Hog Harbour, Santo, 15 January 2002.

95 Ibid.

96 Ibid.

97 Ibid.

98 Ps Kalasakau Urtalo, Talua Bible College, Santo - Lectures Notes 2002.

99 Ibid.

100 Wilson, p. 26.

101 Ibid.

102 Sandy Ishmael, personal interview (Malvatumauri Council of Chiefs) 17 September 2003.

103 Ibid.

104 Ibid.

105 Peter, p. 1.

106 Ibid, p. 2.

107 Connell & Lea, John, p. 96.

108 Ibid., p 23.

109 Ibid., p 23.

110 Ibid., p 33

111 Green, p. 17.

112 Tait, p. 5.

113 Ibid., p. 18.

114 Taylor, p. 37.

115 Ibid, p. 7.

116 Green, p. 25.

117 Speide, p. 298.

Masia Nato

Stanley Ure

Christopher Iawak

Kute Daniel

Amanrantes John Fred

Kaltang Kai Merak

Peter Lai

Urick Lui

Sheila Yamsiu

Martin Namel

Simeon Tavui

Wilson Billy

Kalmatak Ian Tino Sope

Worai Kalsakau

Gideon Paul

Shem Tamara

John Leung

John Riches

Graham Path

William Bice